MW01069303

Other Books by S. Daniel Abraham

Peace Is Possible: Conversations with Arab and Israeli Leaders from 1988 to the Present

EVERYTHING IS POSSIBLE

Life and Business Lessons from a
Self-Made Billionaire and the
Founder of Slim-Fast

S. DANIEL ABRAHAM

WITH

JOSEPH TELUSHKIN

Newmarket Press • *New York*

This book is published in the United States of America.

First Edition

ISBN: 978-1-55704-850-9 (hardcover trade edition)
10 9 8 7 6 5 4 3 2 1

ISBN: 978-1-55704-918-6 (hardcover expanded edition)
10 9 8 7 6 5 4 3 2 1

Library of Congress Cataloging-in-Publication Data
Abraham, S. Daniel.
  Everything is possible : life and business lessons from a self-made bil-
lionaire and the founder of Slim-Fast / S. Daniel Abraham ; with Joseph
Telushkin.
    p. cm.
  ISBN 978-1-55704-850-9 (hbk. : alk. paper)
  1. Abraham, S. Daniel. 2. Slim-Fast Foods--History. 3. Weight loss
preparations industry--United States--History. 4. Businessmen--United
States--Biography. 5. Success. 6. Conduct of life. I. Telushkin, Joseph,
1948- II. Title.
  HD9675.W444S453 2009
  338.7'66463--dc22
  [B]   2009036589

QUANTITY PURCHASES
Companies, professional groups, clubs, and other organizations may qualify for special terms when ordering quantities of this title. For information e-mail sales@newmarketpress.com or write to Special Sales Department, Newmarket Press, 18 East 48th Street, New York, NY 10017; call (212) 832-3575 ext. 19 or 1-800-669-3903; FAX (212) 832-3629.

Web site: www.newmarketpress.com

Manufactured in the United States of America.

I once got together all my top people, and asked each one, "Who do you report to?" And everybody gave the obvious answer: "I report to Joe," "I report to Danny." And I said, "You're all wrong: You all report to the consumer. That's who we all work for."

—Dan Abraham

For my wonderful parents,
Dr. Samuel and Stella Abraham,
who gave me my heritage, my love of
life, my instincts to always do good,
to always be helpful to others, to treat
everyone equally, to be dedicated to
working hard and to always finishing
what you start.

To my loving children:
Rebecca,
Leah,
Tammy,
Simmy,
Sarah,
Sam.

And to my grandchildren and
great-grandchildren, to whom I
would like to pass on the teachings
of my parents and the
important lessons of my life.

And to Ewa, who has made the past
twenty years so blessed.

CONTENTS

Introduction: An Ethical Will

The word "will," as in Last Will and Testament, generally has one association in most people's minds: money and possessions. The disposition of assets. When people talk about a will, they want to know two things: How much is in it? And who got what? Far more often than not, the will is the final communication between parents and children.

How sad!

The Jewish tradition, the tradition that has shaped me since my earliest days, knows of a second kind of will. In Hebrew, it's called a *tzava'ah*, and it is usually translated as an "ethical will." In it, a person is expected to set down, for his family members and for anyone else who is interested, the life lessons he has learned, the people who have most influenced him, the kind of statements his parents made that he would like his children and grandchildren to remember, the causes that mattered to him and that he hopes will matter to his descendants, actions he's taken in his lifetime that he might regret, and the acts of which he is most proud. A person can also tell, as I intend to do, the story of how I went into business, and made a success out of something that sometimes looked—particularly in those first early years—as if it were impossible. I learned a lot of things along the way, not the sorts of things you talk about in a traditional will, but the very things that form the substance of who I am.

So I, Dan Abraham, now in my eighty-fifth year, and being of sound mind and sound body, would like to share with you—my children, grandchildren, and great grandchildren, my nephews and nieces, my friends, and my readers—what I have learned in more than eight decades of a passionate and, I would like to think, vibrant, dynamic, and exciting life.

I

What My Parents and Teachers Taught Me about Life and Responsibility

My mother, Stella Abraham, was a very religious woman, but her piety became more pronounced as she got older. In her later years, it seemed as if she constantly had a *siddur*, a prayer book, with her. Whenever I called her, or would go out to see her, she always sent me off with the same parting words, "May God give you *gezunt* (health), *parnassah* (a good livelihood), and great wisdom." She would say this to my sister and brothers as well, and later to her grandchildren and great-grandchildren (of whom she had many; my mother died on her 102nd birthday). When I think about that blessing, I realize that my mother picked exactly the right things to emphasize—certainly for me. I've always been driven to work hard at business and at everything I've ever done, and to work no less hard on maintaining my health. A few years ago, when I turned eighty, I had severe back problems, and was in tremendous, and fairly constant, pain. It was hard to find a position in which I could sit comfortably for more than a few minutes. I started working with a personal trainer, exercising three hours a day. Oftentimes, these workouts were excruciating and I used to let out grunts and shouts. But I wanted my health back, and I was grateful to God when I got it. My mother's last blessing was for "great wisdom." I'm not sure I acquired that, but my mother certainly knew the things that mattered.

There was another favorite saying of my mother's: "Don't quit before you finish what you started." This expression was one of her axioms, and I can still hear those words ringing in my ears. While other people might say things like that, my mother lived by these words. And she made me live by them, too. In fact, that maxim once led to an embarrassing situation. At the time, I was a teenager—maybe fourteen or fifteen—and I had started putting out a weekly newspaper, the *Long Beach Beacon: The Brightest Light on the Beach.* A new, really attractive, girl had just moved into our neighborhood. I was very shy, even bashful, in those days—whenever a teacher called on me in class, I would turn beet red—but I finally mustered up the courage to ask the girl for a date to go bicycling with me on the boardwalk. So one Sunday morning, I got on my bike to go out to meet her, and my mother stopped me cold, saying, "Where are you going? You have to finish the newspaper; you have a deadline. The paper is due today and you have to get it out on time."

I didn't give up so easily. "I have a date, Mom, come on!!" I pleaded.

This cut no ice with her. "Get off the bike and do

the newspaper. You started this paper, and you can't quit before you finish what you started."

Oh boy, did that lesson sink in. So I had to go tell the girl that I couldn't ride with her, because I had to finish putting out the paper. Now that I think about it, I probably should have invited her to come back with me and help me do it. Seven decades later, I can still say that that experience, though unpleasant at the time, was one of the great lessons of my life: Never stop working on something before you finish.

As this story suggests, my mother had a very strong work ethic. She needed it. We lived in a fourteen-room home that had a coal stove for hot water and an oil burner for heat. When I say the house had fourteen rooms, it probably sounds as if we were rich. But we weren't. Not at all. Houses were cheap then, and this house, because it was so large, required an incredible amount of work, particularly on my mother's part. She'd be down in the basement for hours, washing clothes and sheets in washbasins, putting the clothes on a grate, and literally rubbing the dirt out of them. Of course, there were no electric dryers in the 1920s and 1930s, so she'd hang the wet laundry on a clothes-line outside.

An older lady, Carmita, used to help my mother. She was very nice, and we loved her, but the truth is she was as much work for my mother as she was help. Even when Carmita's health was good, she was not a highly diligent worker. Then, unfortunately, she became very sick. My mother used to take Carmita to the doctors she had to see, and, later, to the hospital as well, even though we had no car. That was the kind of compassion my mother had for people. She didn't send Carmita alone, but took her by the hand. And when the end came, it was my mother who stayed with her, and was in the room with Carmita when she died.

Years later, I learned that this was a Jewish value. When a person reaches the last stages of life, you're never supposed to leave him or her alone. What could be more lonely and isolating than dying? So my mom stayed with Carmita.

But, as I was saying, Mom was a hard worker, and expected me to be one, too. A lot of my time was taken up with chores. I was responsible for mowing the lawn and washing the windows. In addition, I was continuously running to the store for this or that. One of those errands turned into a traumatic incident for me at the time. My mother had sent me to the store with an empty bottle of milk to get a new bottle. She gave me the exact change needed to buy the milk, and the cost included the two cents' return on the empty bottle. Being a kid, I was walking down Park Street, flipping the bottle up in the air and catching it. But suddenly I missed, and the bottle broke, right in the middle of the street. I got really frightened, because now I was short the two cents to pay for a new bottle of milk. When I arrived at the store, panic-stricken, the grocer told me, "If you bring back the top of the bottle, I'll give you the two cents for it." I ran back to the street, praying, "Oh, God, I hope it's still there." Happily it was, but I remember the fear of being short two cents.

The truth is that that was my training. You don't waste money and you don't lose money because there is none around to waste or lose.

My mother never liked to use medicines. When we got sick, my mother would call up an old family friend, Dr. Samuel Adams Cohen (who was, I believe, a retired general in the army), and check out the symptoms. Unless it was something serious, my mother's course of treatment was simple: tea and chicken soup. And, of course, rest. But not too much. As soon as we were well, it was back to school and chores.

Which, for me, was not all that hard. Whether I was born with it, or acquired the trait from each of my parents, I always liked to work and to make money—even small amounts. Name any odd job you've heard of kids doing, and I probably did it. When I was around ten or eleven, I got a bicycle, and I started to deliver packages for the pharmacy and the flower store. I loved making deliveries because most people would tip anywhere from a nickel to a quarter. Besides deliveries, I would mow lawns in the summertime, and shovel snow in the winter. Twenty-five cents for each job—though, obviously, it was more work to shovel snow. But when you're a kid, nothing is hard and you don't even notice. During the summer, at the beach, I would collect bottles of Coca-Cola that had been discarded on the sand. I would also go over to people who had finished their sodas, and ask them, "Can I have the bottles?" Most people would give them to me, and I would take all the bottles I collected, wash them in the ocean, and bring them to the store, where there was a two-cent return for each one.

I used to give all the money I made to my mom. I knew that every nickel was important, so that seemed like the right thing to do. At that age, there was nothing I wanted for myself that I didn't have.

Doing odd jobs and earning money came naturally to me, though I realize that none of my three siblings was inclined to do these kinds of things. So I guess that my love of business was inherent in me from a pretty early age. Certainly, Mom and Dad didn't ask me to mow lawns for people. There was just something inside that drove me to do it.

Life had a lot of really fun aspects also. Growing up, I used to love to go into our kitchen, remove the top from a pot on the stove, take out some food, and nibble on it. That irritated my mother no end. She used to say, "Stop eating from the pot or you'll be dumb," which, I believe, was a Hungarian expression (her family came from Hungary). What she wanted me to do was sit down at the table and eat properly. Truth be told: To this day I still enjoy eating straight from the pot. Delicious.

My father, Samuel Abraham, was a very warm, loving person, but he also had a very strong character. If my siblings or I crossed the line, he would come down on us. As in most traditional homes, when my mother got angry, she'd say, "I'm going to tell your dad," and that would usually make us shape up. But strictness was only a small part of who my father was. He was actually a very nurturing person. Years later, when we were both working in New York City—he as a dentist and me in business—he'd give me a lot of helpful advice. I always associate the word *nurturing* with my dad.

My father deeply influenced me in other ways as well—two in particular. He was a very generous person. I remember my mother yelling at him sometimes for giving too much money to charity when we didn't have enough for ourselves. On one occasion, my father made a $200 pledge to our synagogue, and my mother was furious. We simply didn't have that kind of money. This was in the 1930s—the depths of the Great Depression—and $200 was a fortune to give away. But my father pledged it, and he gave it, though he couldn't give it all at once.

He gave to individuals as well as institutions. I had a private Hebrew teacher named Simon Solomon. My father had originally met him when he was hired to paint our house. Dad quickly realized that not only was Mr. Solomon a religious Jew, but he was also highly knowledgeable about Judaism. So after painting our house, Mr. Solomon was hired to tutor me in Hebrew, and later to prepare me for my Bar Mitzvah. Over the years, Mr. Solomon became my mentor in many things Jewish.

When my father died some years later, in 1948, Mr. Solomon told me about something he had once experienced with my dad. He told me this story during the week of *shiva*—the seven-day mourning period for my father—and you can only imagine how much it moved me. Mr. Solomon and my father had been walking together to the Long Beach train station. It was a cool day in the fall, and my dad spotted a young boy walking on the street without shoes. My father went over to the boy, who was no more than seven or eight, and asked him, "Why aren't you wearing your shoes today?" The boy said, "I don't have any." My dad took the boy by the hand, walked him into the shoe store, and bought him a pair of shoes. Then he rushed off to the train.

It's characteristic of my father, who was a modest

man, that I learned about this incident from someone else, not from him. More than sixty years later, when my first son was born, I named him Samuel (his Hebrew name is Simcha) for my father. At my son's circumcision, I told that story.

My father did things like this anonymously, and he was always generous. The whole family talked about his warmth and generosity. When it came to wedding gifts, he would always give the most he could, and people invariably appreciated that.

My father was the first person who made a business loan to me. I mentioned earlier that I had this idea to put out a newspaper. But I needed a mimeograph machine (try explaining what that is to a young person today!), and it cost $25. No way I could get my hands on such a sum. So my father loaned me the money to buy a used mimeograph machine. As old and as beat up as it was, I can still smell the ink on it. I used to make stencils, put them on the machine, take the ink and slop it over the pad and behind the stencils, and then roll the paper through the press and print my newspaper. It was a one-man operation. I not only wrote the paper and printed it, I used to deliver it, free of charge, to every house in Long Beach. Later, a friend helped me do this. I earned money by publishing ads from local stores.

As for the loan? I paid my dad back twenty-five cents a week for one hundred weeks—almost two years. I can't say that I have ever made a business loan on quite such non-onerous terms.

My father's lesson was as important as my mother's adage, "Never stop working on something before you finish." Even though it was only a quarter a week, my father fully expected that I would meet the obligation and pay it back. If my father had just given me the money, it wouldn't have taught me the necessity of earning money to pay off debts. Borrowing money and having to repay it teaches people to be responsible when they're launching a business, and not to spend more than they have. Many years later, I learned that my father's loan was consistent with the teachings of the renowned twelfth-century Jewish scholar Moses Maimonides. In his summary of the Jewish laws of charity in the Mishneh Torah, a code of Jewish law, Maimonides outlines eight degrees of charitable giving. If you ask people which one they think is the highest form of charity, most people believe it's anonymous giving. But Maimonides writes that the highest degree of charity, "exceeded by none," is providing a poor person with a loan that enables the recipient to start a small business, and not be dependent on other people's aid. So even though I was only in my early teens, my father was already training me to be a responsible businessman.

The newspaper, by the way, led to my first encounter with the larger world of journalism, with the newspapers of New York City, to be precise. I had gotten the idea, I don't know exactly why, to interview the mayor of Long Beach. The city wasn't very large, and Mayor Louis Edwards agreed to the interview, probably because I was a friend of his son's. We spent some time together, and he told me his life story. A few days later—I didn't have a chance yet to publish the interview—the mayor was shot. The mayor was coming out of his house in the morning, accompanied by his body-guard. A disgruntled policeman with a grievance against the mayor was waiting outside. He was furious at Edwards for supporting another candidate for the presidency of the PBA. First he shot and injured the bodyguard, and then he killed the mayor.

Everyone in town was buzzing about this and noth-ing else, and it was one of those rare occasions when reporters descended on Long Beach from New York City. Nobody knew anything about the mayor and his background. One big-city reporter heard that a few days earlier this teenager had interviewed the mayor about his life. This reporter—I don't remember which paper he wrote for—sought me out. "I hear you have the mayor's life story," he said. "That's great. I'll give you fifty bucks for it." And I said, "Yes, sir."

In those days, fifty bucks was a fortune. On a typi-cal week, I used to run one-inch ads from local stores on Park Street for a quarter an ad. I'd typically get about six to eight ads, and on a good week, maybe ten. Which came to a whopping $2.50. And even that money was not pure profit. I had to pay for the paper, the stencils, the ink. So as terrible as I felt about what had happened to the mayor, it was exciting to me to earn in one day an amount that normally would have taken me half a year or more to make.

During the years I was putting out the *Long Beach Beacon*, I used to go to the police station pretty much on a daily basis to find out what was new in town. I'd also write about what was happening at the local school—Long Beach High School, which I was then attending—news about the football team, the clubs, and those sorts of activities. But I would also write about national news. I know it sounds pretentious, but it was a very stormy time, particularly in 1940. America had not yet gotten into the war, but Europe was already deep into the conflict, and by mid-1940, France had surrendered and England was fighting the Nazis alone.

In the United States, three powerful groups were trying to keep America out of the conflict. First of all, those who were pro-Communist opposed the war. Stalin and Hitler had signed a nonaggression pact in August 1939 that enabled Germany and Russia to invade Poland and divide it in half. So the pro-Communists (of whom there were a considerable number) opposed going to war against Hitler, because they saw him as Stalin's ally. Then there were German-Americans, many of whom sympathized with Germany, and certainly did not want to see America go to war against the country from which they or their ancestors came. Finally, the best-known opponents of America's entry into the war were those affiliated with the America First organization, committed to an ideology of isolationism and associated in people's minds to this day with Charles Lindbergh. Lindbergh had acquired the status of a national hero in 1927 when he became the first person to fly solo across the Atlantic and into France, and he had remained a national hero in the public's mind ever since. Unfortunately, not only was he sympathetic to the Nazis, but he also believed that the Nazis were much stronger than England, and that it would be suicidal for the United States to get dragged into a war against Germany. At an America First rally in Des Moines, Iowa, Lindbergh gave a highly publicized speech in which he denounced three groups for trying to drag America into the war—the Roosevelt administration, the British, and the Jews. And he warned the Jews that if they succeeded in persuading America to join this conflict, bad things would happen to them in the United States.

This was a fairly potent combination of opponents—pro-Communists, pro-Germans, and the America First Committee. Meanwhile, the group with which I identified was the Committee to Defend America by Aiding the Allies. I was a teenager then, but I understood—both as a Jew and as an American—what a catastrophe it would be if Hitler were not stopped. I wanted Americans to help the English any way we could to win the war against Germany. I wrote headlines in the paper like, "Wake Up, America." Inside I would run editorials supporting the Allies. We shouldn't delude ourselves about the Nazis, I argued, the way Lindbergh and the America First Committee were deluding people. The objective of the Nazis was not just to take control of Europe. They were out for world domination. Once they defeated England, they would come after the United States.

When we delivered the paper—my friend and I would drop one at every home in Long Beach—we would sometimes get into fights with pro–America First types or pro-Communists or pro-Germans. The fights were usually confined to yelling, but every once in a while someone would throw a punch. To this day, I am proud that these people opposed me. I've always gotten along easily with people, and have had many friends; that's been one of the greatest blessings of my life. But I'm also proud that I took positions that some people (political extremists and bigots among them) passionately opposed. These people were willing to fight against FDR, but not against Hitler.

There was also a lighter side to life in Long Beach, most notably the beach. As you can guess from the city's name, the beach was a big deal there. From an early age, I became friendly with the lifeguard, a man named Jerry Jervo, who really helped me develop my swimming skills. As I grew stronger, I used to swim way out in the ocean with Jerry. When I became older and there was trouble in the water—for instance, people going far out into the ocean and not being able to get back—I would help bring the struggling swimmers in. I learned from Jerry how to get behind them and push them along with the waves toward the shore, until they could finally stand up and walk out of the water on their own.

Jerry Jervo was the right man to teach me. He had been trained as a Greek endurance swimmer. In Greece, he explained to me, endurance swimmers used to swim from island to island, and they would be in the water, if I remember correctly, for ninety minutes at a time and then rest for ten on a boat that was following. Then another ninety minutes, and ten minutes off. During the break, the swimmers would rest on the boat that traveled alongside them. The winner would be the one who lasted the longest. Jerry told me that these competitions could go on for days at a time.

As much fun as I had hanging out at the beach and putting out the paper, that's how little fun school was for me (at least classes and homework). One of the main reasons was that I have never been one to sit around much. I've tended to learn things by talking with people who are knowledgeable in different areas, and by reasoning things out myself. So school was a bit of a struggle.

This was not the case with my brother Roy, who was three years younger than me and a born student. I can still recall the way he'd stay in his room, one or two books open at all times, doing his schoolwork. Often, my mom would call out, "Danny, I need you to go to the store and get . . ."—whatever it was. And I'd say, "But Mom, I've already done three errands today and I'm playing. Ask Roy." She'd cut me right off: "Roy's studying."

Roy really did have remarkable academic abilities. Later, he went on to Columbia Law School and was an editor of the *Law Review*. Back then, the big law firms were not hiring Jews, but for Roy they made an exception. He was, if I recall correctly, the first Jew hired by Cravath, Swaine & Moore, which was regarded as an old-style, Waspish law firm at that time. I remember him coming home in the early 1950s and telling us, "They're paying me a nice salary—$4,000 a year to start." In those days, that was real money. Later, Roy became a protégé of Telford Taylor, the famed lead prosecutor at the Nuremberg trials, who had gone into private practice. Eventually, Roy became corporation counsel for Olin Matheson. He developed a specialty in legal issues involving pharmaceutical companies, and pushed the company to do some of its production in Ireland, because doing business in Ireland had very favorable tax consequences. He was involved with Olin Matheson's acquisition of Squibb (which later merged with Bristol Myers), and its takeover of Clairol. He had a very successful career.

Unfortunately, Roy started smoking before the dangers of smoking were widely known. He would smoke four packs a day, and by the time smoking's pernicious effects were publicly acknowledged, it was too hard for him to stop. I recall sitting with him in a taxi on a rainy day, and he was smoking up a storm. I was choking on the smoke, and I said, "Roy, put out that damn cigarette." He said, "No, this is a free country. I have the right to smoke." I told him that I was going to open the car window and let the rain come in, along with some fresh air. Boy, was that a tough ride.

I don't want to give the wrong impression. Roy and I were very close. We would go to synagogue together, and we'd also spend a lot of time talking about business. When necessary, I turned to him for legal advice. But I tell this story to illustrate how strong his cigarette addiction was. Despite his contention that this was a "free country," our argument had nothing to do with freedom. Just the opposite—addiction to nicotine.

One of the saddest events of my life occurred many years after this event—maybe fifteen or so. I was still in my early fifties, and Roy had just turned fifty. At the time, in 1977, I was living in Israel. It was the holiday of Shavuot, and the phone started to ring. My mother-in-law was visiting us, and the phone just kept ringing. Normally, we wouldn't answer the phone on the Sabbath or Jewish holidays, but I finally said, "Something is wrong. I've got to answer the phone." And that was

how I learned that Roy had died. He had been hospitalized with a heart attack. That day, he had walked out of
his hospital room to smoke in the hallway, where he
collapsed. A brilliant man, a wonderful and loving husband, the father of two sons, and a loving
brother—dead because of his need for eighty cigarettes
a day. I still miss him.

Anyway, to go back from that painful recollection to
happier times. As should be clear, I was not the academic in the family. I did just enough homework to
get by, but no more. In addition, as I mentioned earlier, I was very bashful in those days. If a teacher
called on me, I'd have trouble speaking up. One of my
teachers, a man named Mr. McDonough, taught me
an important lesson about myself. "Danny, you're sitting there like a man with a sword dangling over his
head, held to the ceiling by a thread." He meant that
I was always scared that he was going to call on me,
and that the sword would drop. And he was right.
Even when I knew the answer, I never raised my
hand. If I was called on, there was a good chance that
I would become tongue-tied and unable to answer
correctly. I had no problem speaking one-on-one or
even to two or three people. But when a teacher
posed a question or asked for volunteers to raise their
hands, I would put my head down so that the teacher
couldn't catch my eye.

I'm not so bashful anymore, but I'm still not comfortable speaking in front of groups. First of all, if I say
something, I want it to be something that people will
learn from. Most speakers don't convey much of sub-

stance, which is why most talks, in my view, are a waste of people's time. And I certainly don't want to run the risk of wasting anyone's time.

Other than learning reading and basic arithmetic in grade school, and learning to type in high school (that was certainly the most useful course I took), there was little practical knowledge I picked up in school. Except for one lesson from a teacher named Mr. Greenberg—I think his first name was Ike. Mr. Greenberg taught medieval history, and I can't say that I recall much from his class. He was a very tall guy—I think he had been a basketball player—and a bit idiosyncratic. He liked to do funny things in class, like roll up pieces of paper into little balls and aim them at wastepaper baskets he had placed in the four corners of the room. I can still see him in my mind's eye standing on a desk one day, shooting baskets and offering us his explanation of how the world works. "If you never remember anything else from high school, if you never learn anything else, remember this one thing: An organized minority can always overthrow a disorganized majority."

Nothing I ever heard in school, and few things I have ever heard since, affected my view of the world so deeply. Mr. Greenberg's remark really is a truism of life. For example, an army is an organized entity and it can always overthrow and take control over a disorganized majority. An army goes in with guns blazing, and it's organized to do what it has to do; a disorganized civilian population can't do anything about that. Another example: An organized man with a gun goes into a store and he knows exactly what he wants. So he tells everyone: "Lie down on the floor, take out your wallets and jewelry, and throw them in the aisles, or I'm going to shoot you." They all lie down on the floor, throw their valuables in the aisles, and the guy with the gun picks up all those valuables and leaves the store. He is an organized minority of one.

The only way you can defend yourself against an organized minority is to become an organized entity yourself and get people to join forces with you. This can be done for good causes, though it is commonly done for evil ones. The Nazis went into the streets with trained storm troopers, and intimidated the entire German society into submission. The Jews, of course, were their main victims, and they were simply not organized enough, and eventually not big enough, to overcome the Nazis. So the Nazis, a group that started out as a very small but highly organized minority, ended up taking over and dominating the much larger, but disorganized, German society.

It's understandable that most normal people wouldn't want to organize into a violent, militant group. Most of us concentrate on business and making a living, caring for our families, handling matters as simple as shopping for food—in short, just living our lives. That's why, if members of a particular group are bent on disrupting that life, it's very easy for them to do so, because they are organized for that purpose.

This lesson even resonates when I read the Torah portion each week in synagogue. Genesis 14 recounts how Abraham, together with 318 trained men, went into battle against five kings to rescue his kidnapped nephew, Lot. Most likely, each of the kings he confronted was not fighting in concert with the next king, so Abraham and his troops were able to defeat them one at a time. Why? Because Abraham's men were trained, and they were organized.

Amazing how this one line of Mr. Greenberg's, which I heard almost seventy years ago, has stayed with me. A few months later, with Mr. Greenberg's words of wisdom and the ability to type, I graduated from high school, and shortly thereafter had my next learning experience, one that affected me far more deeply than my twelve years of schooling—serving in the U.S. Army.

II

What War Taught Me about the Insanity of War

I can't think of many things that had as deep an impact on my life as my army experiences during World War II. There was a universal draft at the time, but I could have avoided army service if I had wanted to. I was very nearsighted—20/400 vision—and that qualified for a 4F, a medical deferment. I suppose the army didn't want legally blind soldiers running on a battlefield firing weapons. So I was told straight off, "You're borderline. If you want in, we'll take you. If you want out, we'll give you a medical deferment."

I was eighteen at the time and my country was at war. There was no way I wanted to avoid fighting the Nazis or the Japanese, who had attacked America at Pearl Harbor.

I remember my surprise at the advice offered me by Mr. Solomon, my Jewish studies tutor and the man who had prepared me for my Bar Mitzvah. He was a very warm person, and deeply pious. We had always remained close and just before I went into the service, he told me, "Danny, when you go into the army, don't worry about Shabbes,* don't worry about tefillin,† don't worry about keeping kosher. Just come home alive."‡

I think I understood what he was thinking. As long as I made it back alive, I would have the rest of my life to keep the rituals of our tradition. To this day, Mr. Solomon's advice symbolizes for me much of what makes Judaism such a wise religion. It focuses on this world, and on making this world better. I have often pondered the meaning of life and the fact that all creatures in the universe share one common trait, the desire to stay alive. The purpose of life—as I understand it—is to live, to enjoy life, and to create new life through our children.

The day I left home, my mother walked me to the train station. I don't remember my father being there; he had probably said good-bye earlier and gone to work. My mother was crying as we walked. And I said, "Mom, why are you crying?" I couldn't understand it because when you're young you look at your parents and you know they love you, but you don't understand

---

* That's the Eastern European way of referring to the Sabbath, in Hebrew *Shabbat*.

† Tefillin are two small boxes with black straps attached to them, and with Biblical verses inside. Commanded in the Torah, Jewish men are instructed to place one box on their head, and tie the other on their arm, each weekday morning.

‡ Obviously, it's not always possible for a soldier in combat to stay alive. Mr. Solomon just meant that I should avoid taking foolish risks or doing anything that would needlessly endanger my life.

how very deeply they worry about you. I wasn't feeling any fear myself, just a sense of "Wow. I'm finally going." I just deeply wanted to be in the infantry and see action.

I don't recall much about basic training, but when it ended, the army assigned me to the 100th Division in Fort Bragg, North Carolina. There, I was an aide to a lieutenant in charge of providing entertainment for the troops. That was a pretty easy job, but it didn't last long. A girl I knew from Long Beach had invited me to be her date to the high school prom. I got a leave to go home. It was very hectic—I went by train—and during the couple of days I was in New York, I barely got to say hello to my parents. The prom was fun, but I ended up getting back to Fort Bragg a day late. The lieutenant told me: "You went AWOL in a time of war, and this is a serious offense. You have a choice: you can face a court-martial and possibly a firing squad (he actually said this to me) or you can volunteer to go overseas as a replacement for troops who had been killed or wounded in action."

I agreed, gladly—I really wanted to see action— and a short time later I was sent overseas. It was a bad time in the war, the summer of 1943, and we Americans were suffering heavy casualties. I shipped out on a Liberty Ship, part of a convoy of four hundred ships. We would zigzag across the ocean to avoid German torpedoes. After two weeks, I reached Naples, Italy, and was transferred from there to another ship heading north.

I joined the 11th Armored Infantry Battalion, attached to the First Armored Division as an infantryman. I had the distinction of being the first

American soldier to cross the Arno River, near Florence. As an aside, John Kennedy initially became famous because of how he handled his PT boat and saved himself and his fellow sailors. But when he was asked how he became a hero, he answered, "It was involuntary. They sank my boat."

My being the first soldier to cross the Arno River came about in a somewhat similar manner, at least in the sense that it was unintentional. Our sergeant asked us, "Who knows how to swim?"

I raised my hand. I had spent my whole youth in Long Beach, by the Atlantic Ocean, and swimming was one thing I could do. The funny thing is, ever since I had entered the army, the advice I'd always heard was, "Don't volunteer for anything." But when that sergeant called out his question, I didn't realize that he was asking for volunteers. I suppose the other guys did. It's hard for me to believe that I was the only one in the group who knew how to swim.

Meanwhile, the sergeant was pleased to see a hand go up, and he called out to me, "OK, you're going to be the first one to cross, because if the water gets too deep, we know you can swim out." This didn't exactly reassure me. I was a great swimmer in Long Beach, but now I was going to be carrying a full backpack, a rifle, and grenades. Nevertheless, I started to wade in. Thank God the water never got deeper than shoulder high.

After we got across, we found ourselves in a little town right near the river, and very shortly thereafter I had my initiation into warfare. A German plane appeared overhead and started dropping bombs on us. It was by far the scariest experience of my life. We were fully exposed and there was no place to hide. I did what they had told us to do in such a situation: Lie flat on the ground. I remember a thought I had while lying there. I had wanted to see action. Okay, now I've seen it. How do I get the hell out of here? Even now, sixty-five years later, I can still recall the fierce noise the bombs made coming down. One bomb landed very near me; a few feet closer and I would have been dead at eighteen.

Starting on that day and for the next three months—as we fought our way from the Arno River to the Po Valley—I saw all the terrible things you see in movies, but this was, of course, for real; friends getting their arms blown off or, even worse, getting hit by a shell, square on, and blown to pieces. Often, there was nothing left to ship home. You'd see nice young people you'd been joking with an hour earlier laid out on stretchers with a sheet pulled over them, blood dripping down the stretcher. Even after so many years, details from those months of combat are still fresh in my memory.

In the fall of 1943—we had just finished an attack north of Florence and were digging in. Two of us dug a foxhole together, which was usually about six feet long, a foot and a half wide, and four or five feet deep. The general arrangement was that of us would sleep and the other would stand watch. I was on watch one evening when the sergeant came along. "Everything okay?" he asked me.

I told him everything was fine, but I also mentioned that a few days earlier had been the Jewish holiday of Rosh Hashana, our New Year, and that in a couple of days it would be Yom Kippur, the holiest day in our religion. Remarkably within an hour he came back with a note from General Headquarters saying that any Jewish soldier who wanted to go to services and who was not on an attack could attend services in Florence.

The sergeant gave me the note, then added, "I know you're not using this as an excuse for R&R (rest and recreation). I know you really want to go."

After being away for so long from the intensely Jewish environment in which I was raised, it was quite an experience to suddenly find myself in a synagogue again. Most of the attendees were other Allied soldiers, some were Italian Jews, and I also remember meeting some German Jews. They explained that they had gone through the German lines through some kind of underground railroad system that had been organized to help Jews escape. Hearing these people's reports of their wartime experiences under the Nazis gave me my first real knowledge of the horrible things that were happening to the Jews elsewhere in Europe. I know it sounds odd that I didn't know more than I did. I knew Jews were being persecuted, but until I met these German Jews that Yom Kippur I had no idea how bad things were. That might sound unbelievable, but the truth is that when you're a soldier in combat you're cut off from what's going on in the larger world. The only thing you think about is staying alive and staying with your buddies. You didn't know these people until a few weeks ago, but now you'd do anything for them and they for you. That's why soldiers who are wounded volunteer to go back to their units even before they've fully recovered; they have friends there, comrades, their new family. A soldier in combat doesn't spend much, if any, time thinking about bigger issues. All you're thinking about is marching and reaching where you have to go, so you can sit down and rest, and getting to sleep at night so you can relax after a tough day. Then, when they wake you up in the morning, you're just thinking about how you can get another two seconds of sleep before you have to get up.

Yom Kippur passed and it was back to the front. Sometime later, we entered a city in Italy, near Montecatini. By the time we got there, the city had been so badly damaged that all the residents had fled. Inside the city, there was no running water, so all we had available was what we could bring in. To avoid the German shelling, we quickly took over an empty house. But with no running water, the toilets weren't working, so we still had to go outside and expose ourselves to the shelling. Finally, we got the idea to take over the house adjoining the one we were occupying, and use that house as our latrine. It sounds disgusting, but war makes you do many disgusting things.

One time, I was sitting on the windowsill of our house eating out of my mess kit, with flies landing all over my food.

For a few days, life continued as usual. In fact, better than usual because the Germans finally started withdrawing. That gave me some time to go out into the countryside surrounding the town. I met a young Italian girl—I was all of nineteen, she a few years younger—who was very good-looking and very sweet. She invited me to her home for dinner, and her mother prepared chicken cacciatore. It was delicious and, as you can imagine, a home-cooked meal really outclassed the food in our mess kits. But all of a sudden I had the uncontrollable urge to throw up. I ran out the back door, the poor farmer right behind me. He saw me vomiting and felt terrible, thinking that the food his wife had prepared had caused my illness. I made my apologies, and quickly returned to my unit. The company medic gave me a saccharine pill. That's what the army dispensed in those days to relieve sour stomach upset. But it didn't help. I continued vomiting, and was sent to the local hospital. When they couldn't do anything for me there, I was dispatched to the large army hospital in Naples, where I ended up being confined for three months. The flies had done their job. I had infectious hepatitis.

As awful as the nonstop vomiting was, being out of combat might well have saved my life. But I say that now, only in retrospect; at the time I was very uncomfortable.

Once my illness started to subside, life in the hospital proved pretty relaxing. We used to sit on each other's beds and play cards for hours at a time. One of the memories that sticks with me was of an early encounter I had with bigotry. It seemed insane then, as it still does now. A bunch of us were sitting on one guy's bed playing cards and the nurses started bringing lunch around. The guy on whose bed we were sitting turned to a black soldier—one of the guys playing with us— and said, "Get off my bed." The black soldier got up and walked away; I don't even remember him reacting. When another soldier said, "What the hell was that about?" the first soldier answered, "I won't let a nigger eat on my bed." I just remember thinking how crazy this guy was. We were all sitting on the same bed playing cards together—that was fine. But he wouldn't let the guy sit on his bed and eat. Bigotry is sure a strange bedfellow.

By the way, that was not my only card-playing experience in the army. Another time, I was taking a train back to Reims after having been in Paris. The train had many small compartments, and mine had just me and one other soldier. He asked me, "You want to play some cards?"

I said, "Sure, let's play."

We started playing poker and very soon he was beating me handily. I didn't have a lot of money to begin with, and finally I said, "Okay, enough."

He then said to me, "You look like a nice kid, so let me show you something." He picked up the deck, and showed me various ways he could manipulate it. "I'm a professional, and I make sure to give you the hand I want you to have, even when you cut the deck." He then offered me the deck, and I cut it. But he had arranged the cards so that I got what seemed to be a wonderful hand—two aces—only he had three kings. I still have no idea how he did this. But he had me cut the deck a few more times, and each time he ended up with the winning hand.

Once I realized what he had done, I said, "Okay, you cheated, give back the money I lost." He shook his head. "That lesson I just taught you is worth more than the money you gave me." Then he threw in another lesson for free: "Don't play cards with strangers."

Ever since that experience, I have assumed that most of the consistently winning card players are professionals, and many of them—I don't know how many—cheat. His last lesson did stick with me. I don't think I've played cards for money with any strangers ever since then. He was right. The cost of the lesson was well worth it and anyway he was bigger than me.

That whole experience was like the lesson the writer Damon Runyon claims the gambler Sky Masterson was taught by his father when he left home: "'Son,' the father said, 'no matter how far you travel, or how smart you get, always remember this: Some day, somewhere, a guy is going to come up to you and show you a brand-new deck of cards on which the seal is not broken, and this guy is going to bet you that the jack of spades will jump out of this deck and squirt cider in your ear. But son,' the father says, 'do not bet him. For as sure as you do you are going to get an ear full of cider.'"

Meanwhile, back at the hospital there was not a whole lot to do, which was hard for me because I like to stay active. So I was pleased when a doctor there, an Irish guy and a fellow New Yorker, said to me, "Why don't you come around with me to the wards, and take notes as I visit the patients?" I followed him around, and wrote down whatever he dictated. What struck me as we went around was something that wasn't widely reported at the time—the large number of soldiers suffering from so-called "shell shock" or "battle fatigue" (later dubbed post-traumatic stress disorder, or PTSD). That whole subject got some publicity later on when General George Patton very cruelly slapped a hospitalized, battle-fatigued soldier, and yelled at him that he was a coward. But few Americans back home were aware of how emotionally damaged so many of the soldiers were. I could understand how they got this way, recalling my own terror and the terror of the soldiers around me when we had been bombed, shelled, and shot at. But some of the cases I came across in the hospital were quite extreme. I still remember one soldier with a tongue depressor in his mouth to keep him from swallowing air.

I was even more surprised to learn that some of the hospitalized soldiers had gone berserk for reasons that had nothing to do with battle experiences. What had sent them over the edge were family issues. In several cases I heard about, a soldier learned that his wife had become romantically involved with another man because he had been away for so long. The soldier totally cracked and became violent.

One of the things that helped sustain me during my army years was the mail contact with my parents. The army did what it could to get us mail from home, even when we were on active duty. They understood how good this contact was for soldiers away from home. And it was more than just letters that we received. My dad always made sure to send along some Lipton's Noodle Soup. I still remember the pleasure and joy I experienced eating that soup. It was delicious—particularly in comparison to the boring army food—and I suppose a lot of the joy had to do with it being a taste of home.

While I was in the hospital, an eye doctor examined me for new glasses and when he saw my prescription, he said, "What the hell are you doing in combat? You should be on limited duty, not combat." Unlike the day I entered the army, I was now relieved to hear this diagnosis. Earlier, I had been gung-ho, wanting to get into front-line combat any way I could. I had long since passed that stage, and it was good to know that my combat days were over.

Sometime later, when the army was preparing to discharge me, I was asked if anything was wrong with me. I knew that if something was wrong with a soldier, the army offered compensation. So I said, "Yes." And when one of the officers asked me what the problem was, I said, "I'm nervous."

"Were you in the front lines?"

"Yes, I was in the infantry."

"Were you ever in the hospital?"

I told them I had been and they said, "Okay."

I was discharged shortly thereafter. Later I learned that I had been given 50 percent disability, which entitled me to some $50 a month for a few years after the war.

Thinking back, I've always been proud that I fought in the Second World War. It was a war that needed to be fought. Hitler wanted to rule the world, and the Japanese had unleashed a vicious surprise attack against the United States.

But pride is not the only emotion I feel. Seeing what goes on in war—the thousands and thousands of deaths that leave behind broken families, healthy people saddled with lifelong and sometimes crippling disabilities—convinced me that though it sometimes is necessary, war is almost always insane. I wonder if I would have come to that conclusion had I not seen the horrors of even a just war firsthand.

So it's a bit of a paradox. I fought in a war that I am proud to have fought in. But I sure as hell don't want my son—or anybody else's son—to ever have to fight in a war. I often think back to the time I was in the King David Hotel in Jerusalem with my friend Ehud Olmert and his wife, Aliza. It was years before Ehud became prime minister; he was then the mayor of Jerusalem. We were looking out the windows of the hotel at the famous wall that surrounds the old city of Jerusalem, and I irreverently said to him, "Ehud, tell me, would you give your life for these rocks?"

He said, "Yes, I would."

"Come on, Ehud," I challenged him. "You're kidding. You wouldn't give your life for these rocks."

"Yes, I would."

So then I asked him, "Is that so? Would you sacrifice your son's life for these rocks?"

He was quiet a minute. "No, I wouldn't."

I added, "But Ehud, that's exactly what we're doing."

That brief exchange explains as well as anything why I have devoted the last twenty years of my life to getting people to gamble on peace—a situation in which both parties can win—and not on war, where even the winners are losers.

They tell a story of a doctor who was meeting with a group of badly wounded American soldiers right after

World War II at an army rehabilitation center. He spoke to them very bluntly: "This year you're a hero. Next year you'll be a disabled veteran. After that, you're a cripple."

We need to find a better legacy to leave our children.

III

Getting Started in Business: What My Two Uncles Taught Me about Partnerships, and What Window Ads Taught Me about Selling

I was discharged from the army in December of 1945. I was allowed to go home for a few days' leave that Thanksgiving with the understanding that I would come back to Fort Dix, New Jersey, to be formally discharged. Thanksgiving 1945 was a remarkable day. It wasn't just a homecoming after three years away, but I was arriving literally on the day of my "younger"* sister Judy's wedding to Dr. Eddie Steinberg. That was the first time I had met Eddie, and he has now been my best friend and really close business associate for almost sixty-five years. I speak to Judy and Eddie almost every day. The wedding was made by my Mom and Dad in the living room of our home in Long Beach with a turkey dinner buffet.

---

* Judy is actually a couple of years older than me, but she likes to think of herself as my younger sister. We have always been very close.

As arranged, I then returned to Fort Dix, received my discharge papers, and was back home by Wednesday. I remember talking to my parents about my future, and discussing with them what in heaven's name I was going to do now. They answered matter-of-factly, "You're going to go to work." I said, "Okay," and sure enough the next day I took the train into Manhattan and went to work for two of my uncles who were producing a pharmaceutical product called Stom-Aseptine.

But all this requires a bit of an explanation. Stom-Aseptine was a family business, owned equally by my father and three of his brothers. The product itself had been created by my father in the early 1930s. Dad had always maintained a small lab in our house in Long Beach, where he would utilize his medical and pharmaceutical knowledge to tinker with and produce different products. The most commercially viable of all his creations was a mucus-membrane therapy. Mucus membranes are the openings in the body, such as the nose, mouth, and other openings. It turned out that this product, a powder mixed with water, was a particularly effective vaginal douche, but oddly enough it also worked as a tooth powder and a mouthwash; at home, we used to gargle with it every day, brush our teeth with it, and we even used it to flush out our ears when we had an earache. My father was particularly proud of this product and called it Stom-Aseptine, the capital letters standing for his name, Sam Abraham.

It was clear to my father that StomAseptine had commercial possibilities, and so my Uncle Isadore, whose practice was far more lucrative than my father's (unlike my father, my uncle, though a wonderful guy, did not treat many patients for free), put up the money to develop the product. Two of my father's brothers had been investing heavily and pretty successfully in the stock market in the twenties. But by the time my father had created StomAseptine, it was the early thirties, and the Depression had hit. Both of these brothers (my father came from a large family and had other brothers as well) went broke and came to live in our house in Long Beach. They also were in need of a livelihood. So the four brothers came to an agreement that these two brothers would take on the manufacture and distribution of StomAseptine, and all four brothers would be equal partners.

Unfortunately, it never worked out that way.

StomAseptine achieved considerable success. At one time, its sales got up to $300,000 annually, a large sum of money in those days. The two uncles involved in the business's day-to-day operations took generous salaries for themselves, but when it came time to share with my father, who had created the product, and with my uncle Isadore, who had provided the financing,* they always said there was no money available. At that time, my father was chronically short of funds, and certainly could have used some of the profits of that company. My father felt particularly betrayed at being

---

* In addition my father and uncle also worked on the wording of the packaging and the advertising. What was so frustrating and unjust was that these two men, who did so much to create the wealth and success of the business, were never rewarded.

treated like this by his own brothers, both of whom had lived in our home, and one of whom had been married there. Finally, after protracted negotiations, an agreement was reached that my father was to be paid $40 a week. But even this sum was itself inadequate and vastly less than fair.

Throughout my adolescent and teen years, I constantly heard squabbles between the four part-ners—my father and Isadore on one side, and these two brothers on the other. This had a lifelong effect on me: I never wanted to work with partners because I had seen for myself that partnerships didn't work. One person has to make the final call. Over the years, I took many relatives into my business, but I didn't want any partners. The experience of StomAseptine soured me on partnerships forever.

Anyway, odd as it sounds, StomAseptine is where I went to work. The only other alternative would have been to go to college. The government had a well-known program, the GI bill, under which any veteran could go to college and the government would pay his tuition. But I had already decided that if I was going to spend the next four years doing any-thing, it should be preparing for what I knew the purpose of my life was going to be. And that was earning a living: making money in some business that would support a family, help my mother and father, and whoever else needed it. I felt the obligation to make a livelihood, what we call in Yiddish, *parnassah*. And since I knew it was going to be from business, not law or medicine, I didn't feel I needed a college education.

Nonetheless, given all the tension between my father and his brothers, I suppose what appealed to my parents about StomAseptine was that it was a guaranteed job. I think my uncles were happy to have me, because I was then, and always have been, a hard worker. Anyway, I started working for them for $35 a week, and I was involved in every facet of the business—making the product, to lifting and carrying the bags of chemicals, including one-hundred-pound bags of sodium borate, sodium chloride, and borax. After I had been there a year, I told my dad (and I wasn't bragging): "I'm doing everything—manufacturing, shipping, and running the factory." From my uncles' perspectives, things were working out fine. But I was bored and frustrated. I used to tell my uncles, "Let's develop another product. After all, we advertise, we send samples to doctors. It would be just as easy to sell two products as one." We also had a natural, easy-to-reach customer base. Because StomAseptine was primarily used as a vaginal douche, we were in constant touch with gynecologists and obstetricians. So I figured if we developed a product that appealed to many of the people in those fields, we could increase our sales greatly. For example, there was a product at the time called Midol, used for menstrual cramps and premenstrual tension. I kept pushing the idea of our company developing a premenstrual pain tablet: "We could call it Stop-A-Cramp or whatever, and send it to the doctors at the same time we are sending them samples of StomAseptine." But every time I tried to push this idea, or anything similar, my uncles were opposed. Their attitude was, "We're happy with what we're doing, we've always done it this way, what we're doing is successful, we don't need to put out a new product, and there's no reason for us to do more or change anything." One uncle always had a negative view of any innovation that I would suggest. The other was a gentler sort of person, but that didn't help. In any difference of opinion between the two of us, he always went along with his brother. Our differences of opinion always revolved around my drive for continuous improvement and his insistence on the status quo.

The person I most shared my frustrations with was my father. "They don't want to put any new products out, they don't want to improve anything that they're already doing, and I'm doing the same thing over and over again." As I write these words, I realize how much of my own philosophy of business—the insistence on developing new products, and continuously improving even successful ones*—was forged in those days.

My father knew the character and personalities of his two brothers, and understood that I needed to have an opportunity, as I expressed it, "to cut loose a little." Dad used to read all sorts of journals, including one called *Drugstore News*. In it, he came across an ad for a small company being offered for sale, Thompson Medical, which produced a product called San-Cura Ointment. My father was immediately intrigued by the word *Medical* in the company's name, and set out to learn more about the company itself and about San-

---

* I was deeply influenced by my father's dedication to innovation and perfection as well.

Cura. One of the first things he discovered was that Thompson Medical Company had been founded just a few years before the 1906 creation of the Food and Drug Administration (FDA). The founder was a pharmacist named E. K. Thompson, from Titusville, Pennsylvania. That the company came into existence before the FDA was significant because the FDA soon forbade the use of the word "medical" in a company's name unless the company's leadership was composed of physicians, which was not the case with Thompson Medical. But because its founding predated the FDA, the company was granted "grandfather status," permitting it to continue using "medical" in its name. This was important because it implied "quality" to the consumer.

Dad also learned that the product the company produced, San-Cura, had impressive medical qualities. San-Cura was a topically applied ointment to relieve itching and irritations on the skin. Essentially, it was a petrolatum-based product with phenol as the active ingredient. Phenol is an amazing chemical, an anesthetic that stops itches, kills harmful bacteria within seconds, and promotes healing of skin irritations and minor infections.

When E. K. Thompson died, the business was taken over by his son, and years later bought by an investor, a man named Heyman, who eventually decided that he had no great interest in owning a drug company. That's when he took out the ad in *Drugstore News*, offering the company for sale. Dad contacted Mr. Heyman and proceeded to become more and more interested in the business. At the time, Thompson

Medical was grossing just over $5,000 a year in sales, and Heyman was offering it for one-times its annual sales of $5,000.

Today, of course, $5,000 sounds like an extremely small amount, and even in those days it was not a lot of money to buy a business. But for our family it represented more than we could easily put together. At the time, my father had just taken in a partner in his dental practice. My dad was in his early sixties, but had already suffered a few heart attacks, and his doctor had strongly advised him to take it easy. So he had recently sold part of his dental business to this partner. He now took about $2,000 and put it aside toward the purchase of Thompson Medical. I had about $1,000 saved up from my time in the army, but even with my father's investment, we were still $2,000 short. So my father spoke to my brother-in-law, Eddie Steinberg, who was teaching at Columbia University and who had just opened up his practice as an optometrist. During World War II, Eddie had worked with the Bureau of Ordnance at the navy and had saved up some money. Eddie likes to tell the story of how my dad came over to him at our house and told him, "I know that you are now starting a practice and I have just finished a practice so take it from my experience, when you only work with your two hands you will end up with very little of what you accumulate. But in the business world, there's a chance to really accumulate a lot more money because you can earn from what is produced by many people in addition to yourself. My suggestion, therefore, is that you put whatever money you can into this little company and you'll see years later it's going

to pay dividends, because this business will grow."
Eddie spoke to my sister, Judy, and she told him,
"Don't worry. If my father says it's all right, it's going
to be okay."

Eddie put in the final $2,000, and we were able to
buy Thompson Medical. The business was registered
as "Dr. Samuel Abraham doing business as Thompson
Medical Company." Even though my father always intended to buy the company for me, the reason he
called it that, and not "Dan Abraham doing business
as..." was because as a veteran, the government provided a subsidy for "on-the-job training." As long as
my father owned the business and, technically, I was
working for him, I received $75 a month for training
under this program. Because of my father's medical
and pharmaceutical background, he was considered
qualified to train me. In those days, $75 a month
meant a lot, since a business doing $5,000 a year in
sales did not have money to pay me a salary. Nonetheless, as I shall explain, registering the business under
my father's name, and not mine, was to cause some serious, though happily not permanent, family tension
later on.

Soon after our purchase of the company, I rented a
pickup truck, and drove with Eddie to a warehouse in
New York. We picked up all the boxes that had been
shipped there, most of them half-filled with jars of
San-Cura, and loaded them onto our truck and took it
back to a small loft we had rented in Manhattan at 274
Ninth Avenue, near 26th Street. It's funny, even with
the passage of more than sixty years, I still recall so
many details from those days. Our loft was a walk-up

in a narrow brownstone over a coffee shop/restaurant named Ryan's Rest. When the agent who leased us the loft told me the rent was $80 a month, I gasped, "Oh my God! We can't afford $80 a month, we're only doing $5,000 a year in sales." And even though I realized that the agent's obvious interest was in getting me to rent the space, I also recognized that the advice he gave me was sound: "Danny, remember this: Rent is always the cheapest part of doing business, so don't worry about it. It's the most unimportant expense you will have."

Many years later, when the lease expired on an office we were renting at Madison Avenue and 28th Street, I told Moe Ratowsky, our comptroller and president, that we should move into a more upscale East Side building in the 50s or 60s, a far more expensive neighborhood. When Moe expressed concern about the steep rise in rent such a move would incur, I acknowledged that on purely logical grounds maybe we couldn't afford it yet, but that rubbing elbows with the more successful people we would meet uptown would help us rise to their level of success. Over the years, I have come to believe that if you move into successful surroundings, you will often become more successful so as to fit into those surroundings.

Anyway, moving into that first 26th Street loft was a bit of an ordeal, since the building was a walk-up, and everything, the equipment we needed to produce San-Cura, had to be carried up a large flight of stairs by me. In addition to the many cartons, one of the items I remember carrying up was an old huge copper pot with a burner underneath. We used this pot to heat the petroleum. San-Cura itself was a combination of yellow petroleum, carbolic acid, and one or two other chemicals that I no longer remember. It was originally a doctor's prescription for coal miners' skin problems. Petroleum mixed with carbolic acid, which was an antiseptic and anesthetic, was a great ingredient, but to make it work you had to heat it at just the right temperature. If the mixture got too hot, the petroleum and phenol separated on cooling, and made the product unusable. After some trial and error and frustration, we almost always got it right.

The ongoing manufacture of San-Cura was not only time-consuming, it could also be physically demanding. We used to receive 100-pound drums of petroleum, which had to be carried up the stairs. At the time, I weighed about 140 pounds, and would put the drums on my leg and move up one stair at a time.

In those first months, I spent most of my time inside that loft, since it also served as my bedroom at night. So I would often eat three meals a day downstairs at Ryan's Rest, work in the loft, and then sleep there. Friday night and Saturday I went to my parents' home in Long Beach.

Despite all the hard work, it was also fun. I was happy to no longer be working for my uncles, and to have a business of my own. Also, I was genuinely excited about San-Cura. This was particularly important, because I could never sell something I didn't believe in, and it was easy to believe in this product. Part of what made me so optimistic was that the product had so many applications. It alleviated skin itches and irritations, scalp itch, rashes, athlete's foot, and even psoriasis and eczema.* It was a terrific product, and I felt comfortable marketing it aggressively. I knew it would really help the people who bought it.

At first, we weren't marketing San-Cura directly to stores, but to wholesalers. Our biggest customers were George A. Kelly and McKesson and Robbins in Pittsburgh, and Ellicott Drugs in Buffalo. They, in turn, marketed it to local drugstores. These wholesalers, whose orders came in on a steady basis, had until now been responsible for San-Cura's $5,000 in annual sales, but I knew that if we wished to expand sales we—and we in this case meant me—would have to start selling directly to retail drugstores as well.

A short time later, I made my first road trip. My parents didn't have a car, and I certainly couldn't afford one, so I hitchhiked from New York City to Pittsburgh. Then, after doing business there, I hitchhiked through every little city between Pittsburgh and Erie. I must have stayed at every fleabag hotel in western Pennsylvania at $1 or $2 a night. I'm ashamed to say it, but I had to sneak out of one hotel because I didn't have the two bucks. I don't remember exactly how that happened. I probably had expected to sell some San-Cura at the local drugstore and hadn't suc-

---

* Unfortunately, some years later, the FDA forbade the use of phenol in skin products, claiming that it could cause burning sensations and irritations. In all the years we distributed San-Cura we had never received such a complaint, and I suspect that the FDA, not for the first time nor the last, was overreacting. At the time of the FDA ruling, we replaced the phenol with benzocaine, which worked as an effective anesthetic, and with an antiseptic antibacterial agent.

ceeded. So while the front-desk guy was busy talking to a customer I had my bags in my hand and I walked down the stairs and passed him. But I put my right name and address on the registration so I figured if he wanted the $2 he could send me a note, which I didn't get. Anyway, I'm ashamed of what I did to this day, but I'm just trying to convey a sense of how broke I was.

On these trips, I used to go to every little city that had a newspaper (small local papers were much more common in those days than they are today), and one or two drugstores on the main street. In each city we would run a one-inch ad, identifying the various ailments San-Cura could help cure, such as athlete's foot, scalp itch, and psoriasis. I would then stop in at the drugstores and try to get them to order San-Cura or to increase their order.

The business grew slowly in that first year, going from $5,000 at the beginning, to $7,000 a year later (it only grew to $9,000 the following year). I was still in no position to draw a salary, and had to make do with $125 a month—$75 from the government for my on-the-job training and $50 a month for my partial disability.

And then tragedy struck. In 1948, a year after we purchased Thompson Medical Company, my father died. I was home that day—he died on a Saturday— and I still remember the morning of his death very clearly. What woke me up was my mother's screams: "Daddy's no longer. Daddy's no longer." She never used the word *dead* or *died*, but I understood immediately that something terrible had happened. I threw on some clothes and ran out to get help. There was a doctor who lived on the corner and, as I was running, I was thinking, "I gotta get the doctor, maybe Dad could still be helped." I woke up the doctor, and he got dressed quickly and came. By that time, I had run back, and started giving my father artificial respiration, which I was familiar with from my days of working with the lifeguard on the beach.

But it was too late. The artificial respiration didn't work, and the doctor couldn't do anything. My mother's original words had been accurate: "Daddy's no longer here." My father was only sixty-four, but he had a weak heart and now he was dead.

The following day, my dad's body was still in the house (among religious Jews, a dead body is not moved on the Sabbath, and even after the Sabbath ended my mother wouldn't let them take the body away). My mother gathered all of us, Judy, Roy, Jerry, and myself, into the bedroom where my father's body was lying in a coffin. She lifted up the lid of the coffin and, as we all stood around the body, she said, "I want you all to promise that you will always stay close as a family, close to each other as a family." We all promised.

After all these years, I don't have a lot of memories about the funeral and the *shiva*, but I recall that there was an outpouring of love for my father. He was, as I always say, a nurturing person, and not just to his family. He was generous at the synagogue, he treated many poor patients without charge, and at family celebrations he always pushed himself to give the maximum gift he could. I've already told the story Mr. Solomon recounted to me about my father seeing a young boy walking shoeless, and taking him to a store

and buying him a pair of shoes. My father was a wonderful person, and it was one of the hardest blows in
my life to lose him, especially at such a young age.

Unfortunately, in addition to the awful personal
tragedy of Dad's death, his passing had serious economic implications for our family. Clearly, my two
uncles should have just started automatically paying
my mother the $40 a week they had agreed to pay my
father (which was, in any case, far less than they were
drawing from the profits for themselves). But they
were not at all consistent about doing so, and even
threatened to stop making the payments altogether.
Finally, some of my mom's family entered into negotiations with my two uncles, and the agreement they
came to was not one I was happy with. My uncles
promised to pay my mom the $40 a week, on condition
that I return to work for them. I, in turn, would receive
a salary of $35 a week, which is what they had been
paying me when I worked for them a year earlier. Of
course, the last thing I wanted to do was work for my
uncles again, and had Thompson Medical been generating real profits, I would have gladly supported my
mother out of my own pocket. But the business was
not making enough money, and my mother needed the
$40 to cover her basic living expenses. In addition, my
brother Jerry was only twelve at the time, and my
brother Roy was at Columbia Law School, so they had
to be supported as well.

It was a grim period for me, and while I had to give
up the office on 26th Street, I didn't give up Thompson Medical. I moved back home to Long Beach, and
transferred all the equipment to the basement of the

house. During the coming year, I worked for my uncles during the day and kept Thompson Medical alive at night and on Sundays. That also helps explain why sales grew so slowly during those first years.

Being back with my uncles was as unpleasant as I had expected it to be. I still had ambitions to see any business in which I worked expand, and my uncles squelched every effort I made at new-product development. Seeing that, I tried to develop new products on my own.

It was during this period that a new laxative had been developed, based on a fiber formula called carboxymethylcellulose. This was the first fiber tablet available as a natural laxative and I established a connection with a tablet manufacturer who could produce it. I called the product "Natural-Lax." So throughout this period when I was working for my uncles, I would work on San-Cura at night while also developing Natural-Lax. I then contacted an advertising agency in Chicago—O'Neal, Larson and McMahon—that specialized in developing full-page ad campaigns for drug products, and also helped place the ads in test markets. The agency and I chose a relatively small test market, Toledo, Ohio. I remember taking a night flight from New York to Chicago, telling my uncles that I was sick or something; I needed to give them an excuse so I could get away. I then went to the wholesaler and showed him the full-page ad the agency and I had developed. In the meantime—I don't remember how—my uncles heard about what was going on and said, "How dare you put out a new product and run a full-page ad, when you're working for us?" I said,

"Well, listen, we have to do something to expand the business. If you want it, it's yours. Do you want it?"

They said, "Yes, we'll put it out."

So they did. They ran the ad in Toledo and the campaign bombed.

I don't remember much else about the episode, although I assume they blamed me for the fiasco.

Meanwhile, it was hard to have much of a social life living in my mother's house in Long Beach. So a friend and I rented a room together in Manhattan, down on Greene Street. We each put in $2 a week, for which we got one of the worst little rooms you could imagine, but it had two fairly large beds. On top of everything else, we were living over a used pickle-barrel factory. Eventually, we got used to the smell, but unfortunately, the guy who had the room next to us suffered from consumption. There was only a thin wall that separated our bedroom from his, and he would cough all night. I realize that all this sounds pretty terrible, but the truth is we had fun. We always had a good time down in Greenwich Village, and we always had a girl to go out with. I used to say, it doesn't matter how much money you have: As long as you have a girl with you, you're okay.

By 1949, I had gotten out from under the thumbs of my uncles, and was free to work at Thompson Medical full time. At this point, I was determined to grow the company much more quickly than before, and resumed my road trips to the cities in Pennsylvania and western New York where San-Cura was sold. By now, I owned a little jalopy that I had bought for $50, and which ran about as well as you would expect a car purchased for $50 to run. I don't know how I had the guts to take it all the way on a long trip, but I remember traveling up the New York State Thruway to Buffalo, about four hundred miles, and then slowly making my way back to New York City. At this point, I didn't have the money to sleep in hotels or motels, so I would pull into a gas station, park on the side, and go to sleep. When you're young, everything is possible, and even though I would spend the night in my clothes and stretched out on a car seat, I still recall that I slept well.

Back in New York, we were manufacturing San-Cura at our new small factory and office at 262 Ninth Avenue. We would put this big heater on the stove, heat up the petroleum, put in the phenol, add in the other ingredients, and then pour the liquid petroleum mix into bottle fillers. Earlier, we had cleaned out hundreds of one-ounce bottles, which now lined the table. We would go from bottle to bottle with hand fillers (made out of galvanized steel), and fill each bottle up to its neck with ointment. I was working with one helper, a very nice guy named Richard Rawlins, an African-American who was incredibly loyal, pleasant, hardworking, and a good friend. He used to invite me to his home in Harlem and I would go up and visit. There was a point when the business started to thrive, and Richard brought in his nephews and his aunts to help out at the factory. Unhappily, some years later he was stricken with cancer. I remember visiting him in the hospital; it was terrible to watch such a fine man waste away.

As I noted, our sales did finally start to take off. And the process by which it happened taught me a lot about how to run my businesses in the future. I had long understood that if San-Cura were to grow, consumers had to know about it. Even though San-Cura was the best possible anti-itch ointment on the market, its sales would not increase if its existence remained unknown. So, I once again approached an advertising agency. It was run by a man named Ken Rader, and it was very small; indeed, the company's name was Ken Rader Advertising. I showed Ken the one-inch ads we'd been running in local newspapers in western Pennsylvania. He looked at them, and said, "Listen, the next time you go into a store, why don't you enlarge one of these ads onto an 8½-by-11-inch piece of paper, and tape it onto the drugstore window?" I followed his advice, and that's how I came up with our first 8½-by-11-inch window sign. I remember those signs very well. I must have put up thousands of them. They read, "ITCH relieved in 1 to 3 seconds or your money back." In the beginning, we printed these signs only in black; later on we went to red and black.

Very soon I came to realize the potential of these window signs to expand and transform our business. I was in my $50 jalopy, rumble seat in the back, returning to New York from Erie, Pennsylvania. It had not been a successful trip, and I now found myself traveling on the Pennsylvania Turnpike and broke—really broke. I didn't even have the money for gas to get me back to New York. This was in 1950, when people weren't paying with credit cards. It was November or maybe early December. I remember the time of year because during the month before Christmas, the post office would hire large numbers of temporary workers to help out during its busiest season. Because I was so short on cash, I was looking forward to putting in many hours over the coming weeks to bring in some supplemental income. Anyway, while I was puzzling out how I was going to make it back to New York, I saw a drugstore called Conti's Pharmacy near one of the exits on the turnpike. I had a lot of San-Cura ointment in the back of my car, and since it was a popular product in western Pennsylvania, I knew the pharmacist would recognize the name. I went in and said to him, "I'm selling San-Cura ointment. I have to get back to New York where our headquarters are. I don't have any money at all on me, but I have three dozen bottles of San-Cura in my car. Could I give you the three dozen for $10, and I'll put up signs on your windows and you'll sell them out fast." I don't know how confident the pharmacist was that he would sell thirty-six bottles of San-Cura "fast," given that anti-itch ointments were not thought of as fast-selling items. But, whatever he was thinking, he took pity on me, and accepted my offer. He gave me the $10 in cash, and cash is what I needed so that I could buy gas. Before I left, I taped up 8½-by-11-inch signs all over his store windows. The store windows made the drugstore look like an itch stand. I then left him a stamped, self-addressed postcard, and told him that when he sold out of the three dozen, he should write me, and I would arrange to send him more. I got back to New York and just a few days later I got a postcard, "Rush three dozen San-

Cura ointment, Conti's Pharmacy." I remember thinking to myself, *Wow! This is amazing! Normally, San-Cura sells a piece or two a month in a store, and now it sold over thirty pieces in a few days.* So I sent him a letter, "Mr. Conti. Thank you for your order. I'm shipping it today, and it will be billed through George Kelley Wholesale Drug Company. Could you please tell me what made the product sell so fast? Your pushing it [in other words, the pharmacist recommending it]? The one-inch newspaper advertising? Or the window signs?" I enclosed a self-addressed, stamped postcard. He quickly sent back the postcard, "Window signs, Conti Pharmacy." Nothing else on the card. I was tremendously excited to read that. *What a bonanza*, I kept thinking, if just one store could sell three dozen bottles of San-Cura in a few days with window signs. The possibilities seemed limitless.

I should explain here that there was a distinctive and new element in the signs I was putting up. Signs that had been posted in store windows before then were generally decals that would simply state the name of a product, "Camel Cigarettes" or "Coca-Cola" or something like that. But none of them carried an advertising message for the brand. Now, for companies as well-known as Camel or Coca-Cola, maybe that didn't matter; just announcing that they were being sold at the store would draw customers in. But nobody was going to walk into a store just because they saw a sign saying "San-Cura ointment." But when we included a message, such as "San-Cura ointment. Relieves itch in one to three seconds," there was a very good likelihood that anybody walking by who suffered from an itch would go inside to check out this product. As far as I know, nobody else was putting up signs like this with advertising copy.

Over the coming weeks, all I could think of was, *How am I going to take advantage of this big breakthrough?* It was during those long hours that I was working at the post office during the pre-Christmas rush, doing work that others might have regarded as drudgery, that the idea occurred to me of how to expand San-Cura sales not by $2,000 a year, but by far, far more. It would require an enormous amount of work, but that certainly didn't discourage me—I've been a hard worker my whole life. And it would require perseverance, but I had that, too. You know the old adage in real estate that only three things matter—location, location, location. In business, particularly if you're starting with a good idea, three things matter as well—perseverance, perseverance, perseverance.

Anyway, the idea was ultimately a simple one. I would personally visit every pharmacy in Manhattan—go in just as I had gone into Conti's—convince the pharmacist to stock and sell San-Cura, and then put up a few window signs. I knew how effectively the product worked in stopping itches, so it seemed to me that if we could only get people to try it, our sales would skyrocket.

After my Christmas job at the post office, I loaded my car with packages of San-Cura, window signs, and tape, and drove to the bottom of First Avenue (it was a one-way street going north and Second Avenue was a one-way street going south).

I started downtown at First Avenue and figured I'd work my way straight up north to 125th Street, and then cut across to Second Avenue and do the same thing, until I had covered every pharmacy in Manhattan. I had a game plan worked out that made total sense to me. I went into the first store and said to the pharmacist: "Doc, I have a terrific deal for you. San-Cura anti-itch ointment sells for thirty-five cents. I'll give you two bottles for the price of one, and I'll put up a window sign for you. It'll sell and you'll make 50 percent profit."

I still remember that first pharmacist's reaction as if it were yesterday: "Are you crazy? What do I need another skin itch ointment for? I have a million ointments like that. I don't need another one. Get out of here."

I figured I'd have better luck at the next store. Only I got a similar reception, not just at the second store, but at ten of them. I remember feeling very depressed and frustrated because I knew that if I could get the stores to stock the product, and just let me put up a window sign, they would sell out, and send me back a postcard ordering more. But if they didn't take it, obviously I had no chance at all. I ducked into a coffee shop and I remember sitting there thinking, *What the hell am I going to do now? How am I going to get this thing started?* And then it hit me: If they don't want to put down any money on a product that is unknown to them, I won't ask them to. I marched straight back to the first pharmacist I had visited, and said to him: "Doc, I want to give you two bottles of San-Cura ointment *for free.* Sell them for thirty-five cents apiece and keep all the money. It's yours. I'll even put up the window signs. You'll sell them out fast. Here's a postcard. When you sell them out, send me the postcard, and I'll bring you more at a special price, and throw in two free bottles if you order ten." Two with ten was a conventional and highly popular sales deal at the time.

The pharmacist went for it. The truth is he had nothing to lose. I must have visited fifty stores that day. As soon as the pharmacist agreed to take my bottles, I would go outside and put up not one window sign, but three or four. I wanted to make sure that everyone who walked by that pharmacy saw this little ad. Each flyer was printed on an 8½-by-11-inch piece of paper. I brought along with me cream-colored tape with which to attach the ads to the window, along with a sharp knife to make sure that I cut the masking tape evenly. I wanted everything to look as neat and professional as possible. I still remember how I ran the tape along all four sides of the paper, then pressed down hard with my thumbnail; that way, the flyer couldn't be removed easily. Most importantly, the words on the ad were guaranteed to draw anybody with an itch right into the store: "ITCH relieved in 1 to 3 seconds or your money back. San-Cura relieves itch in seconds, destroys harmful skin germs, and promotes faster healing."

By the end of the first week, I had placed San-Cura in maybe 150 to 200 pharmacies. But I still hadn't received back a single postcard. I was very puzzled. Was it possible that San-Cura did not sell anywhere? And if it had, why was no one ordering more? A few days later I returned to the first store, my third visit now to the same pharmacist. The signs had been taken down.

"Doc, remember I gave you two bottles of San-Cura ointment, and put up a window sign for you." The man was looking straight at me, but it was more like he was looking right through me: "What do you mean two bottles of San-Cura? What are you talking about?" The signs, I could see, were no longer on the window, and the bottles were nowhere to be found. But I wasn't going to give up that easily. Also, it was hard for me to believe that somebody would look me straight in the face and tell me an outright lie. "Remember, I left you with two bottles of San-Cura, and I put a sign up for you, and gave you a postcard. What happened to the two bottles? They must have been sold. I can sell you two more for a half-dollar." He just looked right through me again. "Who are you? I never saw you before in my life. I'm busy. Get out of here." I just kept going on, ignoring the insults. "OK. I'll give you two more bottles again, for free. Can I put the sign up? But this time, if you sell them, please send me a postcard, and I'll sell you more on very good terms." I finally left him with two bottles, walked out, and put up the signs. I figured it was worth leaving him with two more bottles, because I knew that once I'd get his business, I would make a lot of repeat sales.

What was disconcerting, though, was that I got the same response at the next store. And at all the stores after that. It was as if all these pharmacists had rehearsed how they were going to respond to me. Sometimes, when they didn't have the chutzpah to deny ever having seen me, they'd come up with new excuses, such as "Maybe someone stole it, but we certainly didn't sell any." Meanwhile, in every one of the stores, the signs I had so painstakingly put up were off the window. I figured that the moment they sold the two bottles, they ripped the signs off. They didn't want people coming in and asking about a product they no longer had. To this day, I still don't understand why they were so unwilling to order more and give me money for a product they knew they could sell and make a profit on.

So I ended up giving each of them two more free bottles. Eventually, after a few rounds of this, when I finally got them to buy, I had to start out by giving them overly generous terms, like one free bottle for every two they bought.

But still, it was worth it to me. Selling greatly expanded quantities of San-Cura at a small profit sure beat selling tiny quantities at a larger markup. Pretty soon I was covering the whole of Manhattan, and selling an amazing amount of San-Cura. And though the product was very good, what really sparked the sales was those window signs. It's hard for people today to understand the power of those 8½-by-11-inch signs. Today, we have television and the Internet. That's how people find out about things. But television was just starting to catch on then, and, of course, there was no Internet. So when people walked down the street and saw these signs for an anti-itch ointment, it wasn't competing in their minds with dozens of products they'd seen promoted on their TV screens. On some store windows I used to put up so many signs that it looked like the whole pharmacy was an itch store. The pharmacists used to call me "Itch," and I called them, "Doc."

Within a few months, I was covering hundreds of stores in Manhattan, and then I started going into Brooklyn, too.

Meanwhile, a guy named Harry Silverman showed up in my office one day. "I'm a pharmacy salesman in the Bronx," he told me, "and I'd like to sell your product because I've been seeing all these itch signs in Manhattan." So Harry Silverman became our representative in the Bronx, and now we had coverage in what were then the city's three most populous boroughs.

Once the deal in the Bronx came through, I couldn't help but start thinking in bigger terms. The funny thing was, we were still only doing about $75,000 a year in sales, but since I had only been selling at the rate of $9,000 a year a short time earlier, everything suddenly seemed possible.

I also figured that the time had come to bring out a second product, and broaden Thompson Medical's pipeline: Once we were soliciting orders from pharmacies for one product, it wouldn't take much more effort to get orders for two. The first new product we brought out was Gas-Tabs. As the name indicates, it was intended to help people with stomach gas, a perennial and widespread problem, and therefore a product with a guaranteed customer base. The name, I think, was a good one, because it was so descriptive. From the beginning, I thought it had much greater potential than San-Cura. San-Cura was an ointment, and people used only small quantities at a time. They would rub in a little San-Cura, and pretty soon it would alleviate the itch, cut, or irritation. Then they would put the jar away. Most people found that one jar of San-Cura lasted for a year or more. So even though the product worked, we weren't getting the quantity of repeat sales that an effective product—particularly a relatively inexpensive one—should generate. I wanted to launch an item that people would use up much faster, and therefore buy much more often. We started sales of Gas-Tabs with a box of thirty tablets, each one wrapped separately in cellophane. The whole package was very attractive—as an added plus, the separate wrapping of each pill made the box look larger—and we were able to sell it for a dollar.

We created a window sign promoting Gas-Tabs, as we had for San-Cura. This one was pretty vivid and attention-getting. It showed a picture of a stomach half-full with red gas and the tablet coming down to the rescue. Under the picture, there were just a few words: "Gas—relieved fast, in seconds." The sign worked. Very quickly—even faster than I expected—Gas-Tabs was outselling San-Cura. Soon it was time for a third product. This one was Throat-Aid and, as the name suggests, it was for sore throats. It was the first antibiotic throat lozenge on the market. On the packaging and on the window signs, we wrote, "Sore Throat—fast relief."

My intention was to address the most common maladies afflicting people. I knew these products worked, and, just as important, I knew that these maladies were so common that they would generate repeat sales.

But now, with the introduction of Throat-Aid, for the first time—unfortunately, not for the last—we ran into difficulties with the FDA, the Food and Drug Administration. Shortly before Throat-Aid was introduced, a pharmaceutical company introduced a new antibiotic, tyrothricin, specifically for treating sore throats. Suddenly, we were called in by officials of the FDA, who told us that we could not specify that Throat-Aid treated sore throats. Even to this day, their reasoning sounds very odd. A sore throat, they told me, may indicate a cancer, and declaring that Throat-Aid was for sore throats made it sound as if it were capable of treating a much more serious disease than it could. I brought the FDA officials packages of Vick's, a nationally marketed product, which was sold in small boxes of twelve lozenges, and specifically labeled for people with sore throats. And I also brought in bottles of Listerine, which similarly advertised itself for use by people with sore throats.

Their response? "Oh, we didn't see those products. Thank you for bringing them to our attention."

I was really puzzled. "But then, how did you pick up Throat-Aid when it's only available in New York City, and ignore these products which are distributed nationally?"

It was a good question, to which they had no answer, other than, "Listen, we have you now, so you have to change, you have to stop saying 'Treats sore throats,' and we'll get to them." Which, of course, never happened.

I tried to understand what the FDA was doing. The first thing I did was call my brother Roy, a corporate attorney, and ask for a referral to a lawyer who could help me with the FDA. He introduced me to a female attorney—not so common in those days—Pat Hatry, who was excellent. She couldn't do much on this situation, but a few years later, when the FDA tried to shut down my most successful product, she really helped.

Anyway, even with all of Pat's and my efforts and arguments, the FDA wouldn't back down. They had no problem with our continuing to market Throat-Aid, but all we could say about it was that it helped relieve throat irritation; all references to *sore throat* had to be removed from our advertising and packaging. We had no choice, so we did as instructed, and it absolutely killed sales. Which was a damn shame, because it was a genuinely good product, and more effective than both Vick's lozenges and Listerine. In fact, the product was so good that I was reluctant to just give it up. So we continued to sell it for years, even though its sales were very slow. Meanwhile, San-Cura continued to grow steadily, and Gas-Tabs grew even faster.

It became increasingly clear to me that there are a few basic steps involved in growing a business. First, the product has to be effective. With smart advertising, it's not hard to get someone to buy a product once. But to keep customers coming back, the product has to work. San-Cura really did relieve itches, and Gas-Tabs quickly stopped the discomfort of stomach gas. That's why we kept getting repeat sales.

But just putting a good product out on the market is not enough. You have to find effective ways to sell the product, because the more people who try the product the more repeat sales you'll have. That's why you have to package the product attractively, and advertise so that people know it exists.

In addition, not only should your product be better than that of your competitors, you have to sell it for a price that people find affordable. You also need to develop a good team of salespeople who can go out and promote it. And you have to constantly bring new products to market (this was exactly what my two uncles at StomAseptine refused to do, and it's why their business hit a plateau and never expanded). We were doing all this, and our business was finally starting to take off. I remember the year when, for the first time, our sales approached a million dollars—a lot of money in the 1950s.

And that's when the FDA came after me a second time, and almost succeeded in closing down everything.

IV

What I Learned from the FDA about How to Get Along with Authority and How to Fight and Fight Hard, But Only as a Last Resort

It all started during the time when I was still putting up window signs for San-Cura, Gas-Tabs, and Throat-Aid. One day, a man whom I had never met saw me putting up my signs on the drugstore windows. "Are these signs really effective?" he asked me. "Do they sell product?" I told him that they were, in fact, very effective. In retrospect, I should have down-played just how effective they were. The man went on to tell me that he had a product—he didn't tell me what it was—and he was wondering if he should do the same thing.

The conversation sort of slipped out of my mem-ory, but a few weeks later I came to a store, and suddenly I saw another sign there: "Reduce. Lose weight with Special Formula Gum." I remember thinking, "Whoa! Now I have competition for the win-dow space." But things quickly got worse. Before I knew it, the man—I don't recall his name—was tearing down my signs to make room for his. So I started doing the same to his signs. It became a matter of who worked harder and faster.

I soon learned that this new product, Special Formula Gum, was selling very fast. By that time, I was on very friendly terms with almost all the pharmacists to whom I was selling. I was always giving them great deals, like "Buy nine San-Cura and get three for free." One of the pharmacists with whom I had a very good rapport said to me, "Danny, this guy with the Special Formula Gum is doing just great. You should bring out something similar—a gum that helps people reduce."

I was always anxious to develop new products. But this one made no sense to me, as I said to one of the pharmacists who broached the subject: "How can a little piece of gum help a big, fat person lose weight? I'm not going to do it, because I don't want to put out a product that doesn't help people accomplish what they buy it for."

For one thing, I thought it wasn't right to do that. Someone buys a product for a purpose, and if there's no chance it's going to help him, that's like stealing. And it doesn't make sense from a business standpoint. If the product doesn't work, you're not going to get repeat sales, and repeat sales are what keep a business alive, especially if it's a low-price item that you have to sell in large quantities to make a profit.

But month after month, first this pharmacist and then others kept telling me, "Come out with a chewing gum to lose weight. It's really selling." Then Harry Silverman, my salesman in the Bronx, said to me, "Danny, you got to come out with this gum. It's selling like hell."

I kept repeating to each one of them what I had said to the first pharmacist: "How can a small piece of gum help a big fat person lose weight?"

But one day, I started asking the pharmacists the obvious question, which I can't believe I hadn't bothered to ask until then: "Tell me, do the same people come back for it again and again? Does it really help them to lose weight?"

And they told me, "Yes."

To this day, I remember exactly what I thought: *Maybe Dan Abraham doesn't think a chewing gum like this can work. But I'm not the smartest person in the world, so it doesn't only matter what I think. If people are buying this product, and coming back for more, then it must work, and I'm wrong.*

I finally decided to put out a similar product but better, more effective. We checked into the product's formula, and went to Topps Gum Company, whom we hired to produce it. Everyone knew Topps. They put out baseball cards in packages with bubble gum, and they also put out a line of Chiclets. We called our product Slim-Mint Gum. It was a regular gum with good flavor and benzocaine, which anesthetized the taste buds and suppressed hunger pangs. If I recall correctly, our competition, Special Formula Gum, was using methylcellulose to achieve a similar effect.

We gave the gum to Dr. Milton Plotz, a fine physician, for a clinical trial on fifty patients. Dr. Plotz monitored their weight loss, and then published an article about it in a journal called *Medical Economics*. The journal—I don't think it exists anymore—was the size of *Reader's Digest*, and was distributed to doctors. Many doctors tested the efficacy of products and wrote about the results, if favorable, in this journal. Anyway, we reprinted Dr. Plotz's article, and then packed the article into every counter display of Slim-Mint Gum. That way, we hoped the pharmacists would read how effective the product was and recommend it to their customers.

Normally, I would have felt very uncomfortable bringing out a product that was so similar to something another company had marketed. But this case felt different. The company's chief salesman—for all I knew he was also the product owner—had not only copied our idea of window signs (at the time, we were the only ones doing it), but he had started ripping off our window signs to get better placement for his. So I felt that he had thrown down the gauntlet by copying our trademark way of doing business.

Suddenly, there were two weight-loss gums on the market, Special Formula and Slim-Mint. And the competition between us grew fierce. He started offering the pharmacists two free packages with the purchase of ten packages, so we matched him. Before I knew it, we were giving away four free packages with the purchase of eight. I used to leave my bag—in which I carried my window signs, tape, and plenty of samples—in the pharmacy floor area with the pharmacist. I would take out the signs and tape to go put up window signs, and leave the bag behind. Most of the pharmacists, I found, would look into the bag and take out some samples, which they would then sell. I knew what they were doing, and they knew that I knew what they were doing. It made me very popular with them, and I preferred to do it that way rather than to have to offer an even bigger discount. But my competitor kept offering the pharmacists bigger and bigger inducements to buy Special Formula. Finally—I think it was at a point when we had started to outsell him— he was offering the pharmacists, "Buy one dozen and get an extra dozen free." I didn't try to match that, because at that point it would have become a money-losing proposition. Some of the pharmacists would pressure me, asking me how I could expect them to turn down the wonderful offer my competitor was making them. And I would say, "Listen, do you want to buy product or sell product? If you want to sell product, then buy Slim-Mint Gum, because it sells faster, and even if your profit on each individual item will be a little lower, in the end you'll sell a lot more product and make more money."

My instinct was correct. Special Formula couldn't make money giving away a dozen for each dozen they sold, and in the end the company went out of business. We, however, kept doing very well. And I learned a lesson from that, too. It's sort of encapsulated in an old joke. A businessman is bragging about how he kept lowering the price of an item he was selling, and sales increased tremendously, 10 percent the first month, 25 percent the second. By the third month, sales were up 50 percent.

His friend asks him: "Did the sales growth just continue?"

"Yeah," the man said. "By the fifth month, our sales were up 100 percent. Unfortunately, though, we went bankrupt."

The truth is you can struggle along on low profit margins—giving away four free for every eight we sold left us with very low margins—and hope that eventually the quantity sold will compensate for the low margins, or that people will like the product so much that you'll eventually be able to raise the price. But the one thing you can't do is sell at a loss. Sooner or later—and it's usually sooner, especially if yours is a small business with few assets—that will drive you out of business. That's why, as I will explain later, even when our company got very big, and small suppliers, competing to get our business, would offer us incredible incentives to buy from them, I always made sure that they were going to make money. It wouldn't be right if people doing business with you didn't also turn a fair profit.

Slim-Mint Gum took off faster than any other product I had developed up until that time. Suddenly, we were selling in the hundreds of thousands of dollars, and were well on our way to annual sales of a million dollars. And then, just as suddenly, a new, and entirely unexpected problem arose. Our sales were going up rapidly, but our profits weren't. One year, profits were up to about $100,000 in the middle of the year—a huge amount in those days—and then when the year ended, all of it had evaporated. I had no idea how that had happened, which was particularly odd since I used to track profits and losses very carefully. It became clear that I was doing something self-destructive that was sabotaging my success. I thought about it a lot, and then decided to confer with Dr. Saul Heller, a psychiatrist whom I had first consulted after my army years.

This, in itself, is interesting because there were many people from my generation who were still skeptical about the newly emerging fields of psychiatry, psychotherapy, and psychoanalysis. But I was not one of them. Early in my life, just after my army years, I was able to visit a psychiatrist as a World War II veteran. That was when I became acquainted with Dr. Heller, who went on to have a profound influence on my life. One of the important lessons Dr. Heller taught me was that when you want to do something that is within reason and you don't succeed, it is because your subconscious is controlling your conscious. It was Dr. Heller's belief that unless the conscious and the subconscious were in harmony, the subconscious would always control the conscious. When the two are in harmony, however, it is easy to do what you want to do. You would have thought that that would be the case here. Obviously, my conscious mind was happy making a profit of $100,000, and I could think of no possible reason that my subconscious mind would want me to lose that profit.

I went to see Dr. Heller and told him what was going on: "I really want to make a profit, and I am making a profit in June, but by the end of the year, it's gone. Maybe my subconscious doesn't want me to make a profit for its own reasons, and I need to figure out what they are."

I ended up going to Dr. Heller for several months. During one visit, I remembered a recent dream and I told him about it. In it was a memory from my childhood. When my mother used to bake cakes, she would put them out to cool on the kitchen window. Our basement had a slant-board over it, and I used to scamper up the slant-board and put my hand on the top of the cake and pull off some crumbs. It was fun to do, and the crumbs were delicious. That morning, when I woke up, I said to myself, *Wow, why am I thinking of this in the midst of all that's going on in my life?*

Then, a few days later, I had another dream set in our Long Beach house, only this one was more disturbing. In that dream, I was running out of the house with an attaché case. Our house was a half-block from the corner and the cops were chasing me. I was moving ahead of them when all of a sudden my feet, though churning, became frozen in place. I couldn't move, and the police were closing in fast. I woke up again, this time very uncomfortable, and thinking, *What the hell is going on?*

Under Dr. Heller's prodding, it soon became clear what was going on. As I described earlier, when we purchased Thompson Medical, my father put in about $2,000, my brother-in-law, Eddie Steinberg, put in another $2,000, and I put in all the money I had saved from my army salary, which came to about $1,000. My father wanted the business purchased for me because he understood how miserable I was working for my uncles, and he wanted me to have a business of my own. I was only twenty-two at the time, and my brother Jerry was then eleven. There was an understanding between my father and me that, while the business would be mine, I would share some of the profits with my family.

When it came time to register the business' name, it was listed as "Dr. Samuel Abraham doing business as Thompson Medical Company." As I explained earlier, the reason it was set up that way, and not as "Dan Abraham doing business as Thompson Medical Company," is because if my father owned the business and I worked there, I could qualify for the $75 a month on-the-job training under the GI bill. All this was perfectly legitimate and, in addition, the $75 a month was absolutely necessary to the company's financial survival. Thompson Medical's sales were so low that there was no way I could draw any salary from the company. That $75 a month was my income, along with the $50 a month in partial disability I received from the army.

Unfortunately, my father died a year after the purchase of Thompson Medical. My brother Jerry was only twelve then, and didn't have much interest in the business at that time. Nor did he have much interest in it in the coming years. He was still very young, and the business was very small in any case. But by the mid-1950s, when the business was finally starting to take off, Jerry was considerably older, and he had some strong views of his own concerning the ownership of Thompson Medical. He felt that he should be an equal partner with me in the company. Jerry argued that the company was our father's inheritance to his children. Therefore, Jerry felt that the company should be divided equally between me and my three siblings.

I knew, however, that though the business was registered in my father's name, it had always been my father's intention for the business to be mine. I also knew that I would have struck out on my own, and never taken over Thompson Medical, if I were going to have partners. Having partners is precisely what I did not want. Nevertheless, sitting in Dr. Heller's office and analyzing my dreams, it was clear that there was a nagging feeling gnawing at me. Was I a thief? Certainly, the dreams I was having—picking crumbs from my mother's crumb cake and running to the corner with an attaché case from my parents' house—suggested that I was taking something from my family. On top of this, there was this sensitive family history involving the two brothers who had treated my father so badly.

Anyway, once I realized the source of my discomfort and guilt, I arranged with Jerry and my mom for the three of us to go to a rabbi we all knew and respected, Emmanuel Gettinger. He lived in Manhattan, was a highly esteemed scholar of Jewish law, and was regarded as a friend by our whole family. We figured: Let him hear the claims of all sides and decide. He heard Jerry's arguments and mine, and ruled that my claim was legitimate. It was clear, he said, that my father intended Thompson Medical not as an inheritance for the whole family, but as a business for me to own and run. When I incorporated the business, I gave my mother a 6 percent share in the company and I also gave a 6 percent share to each of my siblings—Judy, Roy, and Jerry. By doing so, I was fulfilling the promise I had made to my father—that I would share the profits with the family. I had a very close relationship with my dad, and I wouldn't fool around with that for anything, even though he had passed away. So I was fully content to give away ownership of a quarter of the business, as long as I retained what I wanted, which was control of Thompson Medical, and thereby the ability to avoid the complications of dealing with partners.

Once this issue was cleared up, profitability was quickly restored. It really had been my subconscious sabotaging me, and it was good to have my conscious and subconscious working again in harmony.

The late 1950's proved to be a good period for the company. We started taking Slim-Mint Gum national, or at least semi-national, in a much bigger way than we ever had done with any previous product. Citing Dr. Plotz's article—along with his reports documenting that one patient had lost seven pounds in a week, another nine—we took out a full-page ad in a Chicago newspaper. One of the places we were selling the product in Chicago was at the Walgreens Pharmacies and, with the company's permission, we reprinted our ad and pasted it on their windows.

Shortly thereafter I got a call from Charlie Elson, a dear friend in Chicago, and the merchandise manager for Walgreens' drug department. The FDA had come into one of the company's stores and seized five cases of Slim-Mint Gum. They took particular exception to our ad's claim that you can "Eat what you want, yet lose up to 3, 5, even 9 pounds a week."

We countered that an ad was not under the FDA's jurisdiction; rather, it fell within the purview of the Federal Trade Commission. The FDA insisted that since the ad was in the window of the store selling the product, it was as if we had put it directly onto the packaging of the product, and would be considered labeling.

I called up Pat Hatry, and we immediately headed to Washington. The product was doing very well, and I wanted to settle this quickly. I was willing to accede to any reasonable demand the FDA made. All I wanted to do was to continue to sell Slim-Mint because it was so successful in helping so many people lose weight.

We met with the commissioner—I don't remember the man's name—and, as always, I was as conciliatory as possible. "We believe Slim-Mint Gum is a very effective product, and I believe it should stay on the market. But I'm willing to modify all advertising claims that you think are misleading."

At first, it seemed as if he might be open to our proposal, but then he said: "What about the name? That has to change, too."

I was flabbergasted. "Why?"

"That name implies that you can lose weight with this product, and we don't believe you can. If you want to keep this product on the market, you have to remove all claims implying that this product can help you lose weight, including the name."

"What sort of name would be acceptable?" I asked him.

"You could call it 'Abraham's Gum,'" he said. I still don't know whether he thought he was being funny. Anyway, he probably noticed my look of annoyance, even amazement, so he added, "Look, I have you by the nuts, and I'm gonna squeeze." This was 1959. You didn't expect to hear people in positions of authority speak like that, particularly not in the presence of a lady.

There was nothing more to talk about. We left the office and I said to Pat, "There's nothing for us to do. We'll have to go to court. If I give up on Slim-Mint, I'm out of business."

Meanwhile, when I told Charlie Elson in Chicago

what had happened with the FDA commissioner, he asked the FDA if he could continue to sell and to re-order Slim-Mint. The person he spoke to said, "Legally, you can continue to sell it while the litigation is pending."

Many people in Charlie's situation would have pre-ferred not to antagonize the FDA or get involved in what seemed to be a troublesome situation. But he just said to me, "Send me another order."

Later, Charlie testified at the trial, noting that not only did many customers express to him their great sat-isfaction with the product, but they also kept buying more, a sure indication that the product was working. Needless to say, I was deeply touched by Charlie's friendship and loyalty.

The trial lasted two weeks. In addition to Pat, who was not licensed to practice law in Chicago, we hired a local attorney, George Burdett, who was a wonderful lawyer as well. We could have called in Dr. Plotz as our main witness—his original study supplied the basis for our newspaper ad—but we ultimately concluded that it would be wiser to hire a local doctor to do a second study. We figured that a Midwest physician would be more sympathetically received by a Chicago jury, and also, if the doctor's study supported our claims, then we would have two studies documenting the gum's effectiveness.

Through a connection established by my brother-in-law, Dr. Eddie Steinberg, we found a doctor in Kansas City, Fred Treffer. Pat and I flew out there to meet with him. Ironically, given the study we were going to ask him to conduct, Dr. Treffer turned out to be quite over-weight. Which led to its own funny story.

Pat and I met him at the university hospital where he taught, and then took him to lunch in the school's cafeteria. After a few moments of polite dinner conversation, we came straight to the point: "Would you do a clinical study for us using Slim-Mint with your patients?" Dr. Treffer said yes, and we quickly worked out an arrangement for the study and for payment. Then dessert came. Pat and I had ordered coffee, but the waiter put down a large piece of chocolate cream pie in front of the doctor. It looked delicious, but my own vanity about my appearance kept me from ordering such a fattening dessert. Dr. Treffer cut off a large piece with his fork and, as he raised it to his mouth, I said, "Doc, wait a minute. Do me a favor, and don't eat that pie. Try a piece of Slim-Mint instead." He got red in the face, and glared at me. I worried a bit, because he seemed highly insulted. But he did put down his fork, and put the gum I offered him into his mouth. A few minutes later, when we rose to leave, he still seemed annoyed. He walked in front of us to the elevator, and no one said a word. But while we were waiting for the elevator to come, I got up my nerve and asked him, "Doc, tell me, do you miss the pie?"

And he said to me, "You son of a gun, you know I don't."

That broke the ice between us. Like Dr. Plotz, Dr. Treffer performed the clinical test on fifty patients. If memory serves me correctly, every one of them lost weight, and many lost quite a bit. Dr. Treffer turned out to be the star witness at our trial. After he was sworn in and offered his medical credentials, he presented a chart showing the results of his tests. Each of the fifty patients was assigned a number. Number 21, he pointed out, lost eight pounds over the course of the study, and number 30, ten. Then, he pointed to one number on the chart and said, "This patient lost fifty pounds." Everybody looked dumbfounded, and he then said, "That patient is me." He stood up, I think he was still wearing his old pants with the belt tied very tightly, and he released the belt and showed how big the pants were. He explained that before he tried Slim-Mint Gum these were the pants he used to wear. He even brought along one of his old, much longer belts, and showed it off in the courtroom. As you can imagine, his testimony made a great impression on the jury.

Still, as I noted, the trial dragged on for two weeks. We had consumers testifying, we had rebuttal witnesses, we had a few more doctors and, as I mentioned, my friend Charlie Elson from Walgreens also testified. The FDA brought in a Dr. K, a man whose testimony the government thought would destroy us. (For reasons that will be apparent, I am simply referring to him by the first letter of his last name.) Dr. K claimed to have done a careful patient-based study of Slim-Mint, and to have found it ineffectual when it came to losing weight.

Dr. K's testimony might well have done us in, but we had learned things about him that legitimately cast everything he said in doubt. By a lucky coincidence— the kind that would sound ridiculous if it were in a work of fiction like a short story or a movie—a friend of mine, a stockbroker, had a partner whose wife was a nurse in Dr. K's office. My friend had talked about the case with his partner, which is how he learned that the man's wife worked there. The nurse, it turned out, was extremely critical of the methods Dr. K was using in conducting the study. His approach to the study was sloppy, unscientific, and clearly designed to show Slim-Mint to be ineffective. Most importantly, Dr. K wasn't seeing the patients on a regular basis and weighing them in his office on the same scale each week. Instead, he'd have the secretary in his office call up the patients and ask them how much they weighed. The scales on which the patients were weighing themselves had not been calibrated, and Dr. K's secretary had no idea what the patients were wearing when they weighed themselves or even if they were weighing themselves at the same time of day. For that matter, the doctor didn't know if they even were weighing themselves at all or just reporting a number. Furthermore, when patients come on a regular basis to a physician's office, they are motivated each week to keep using the product they are taking. But because Dr. K was simply relying on phone calls, he had no way of knowing if the patients were even taking the gum, a detail that could easily account for their weight remaining the same, or maybe even going up.

Perhaps most significant of all, Dr. K had a serious conflict of interest. Dr. K claimed to be an expert on helping people lose weight, and used to sell his patients pills that were intended to help them to do so. We knew about this, and sent in our company president, Moe Ratowsky—a man unknown to Dr. K—for a weight-loss consultation. At the end of the visit, the doctor sold him these pills. At the trial, we asked Dr. K about this: "Aren't you in competition with Slim-Mint, and couldn't that be influencing your testimony?"

The doctor grew indignant. "That's ridiculous. Why would I care about some ineffective over-the-counter product?"

At this point, our lawyer produced one of the pills Dr. K dispensed to his patients and asked him if there was any lettering on the pill. He said, "Yes," and our lawyer then asked him, "Could you please read out loud the letters on the pill to the jury?" He read out the letters, and they spelled out his last name. In other words, he, the man making and selling the pills, was also claiming that he could conduct an objective study on a product put out by a competitor.

As good as the impression Dr. Treffer made on the jury, that's how poor an impression this star witness for the government made.

When the trial finally ended, the jury came back and ruled in our favor against the FDA. This was very unusual—for a small company to challenge the FDA and win—and the verdict got a lot of attention, particularly in business publications.

A few moments after the jury announced its verdict, I slipped off with Pat to a small room near the courtroom. I needed to be away from everyone. Once we were inside, I just started crying. This was very unusual for me. I come from a generation of men who don't go around showing their emotions. I've only cried a few times in my whole life. This time, though, was one of them. I said to Pat: "What if we had lost, I would have lost everything. The whole business. My entire future would have gone up in smoke in front of me." And Pat said, "Danny, when you're right and you fight hard enough, you will always win."

That was certainly one of the best pieces of advice I've ever received. It's never good to let yourself be bullied. It is terrible even when you're in the wrong, but it's particularly important to fight back when you're in the right. If you don't, not only do you lose your self-respect, but you may also lose your entire life's work.

Thank goodness that was the last time I had a conflict with the FDA or any government agency. I felt that the best way to resolve issues with the FDA was man to man, in a sort of one-on-one diplomacy, and it worked.

V

The Expansion of Our Business, The Thompson Medical Company

One of the things I came to understand from work in weight-loss products is that while people eat for nutrition to stay alive, they *overeat* for pleasure, and pleasure comes through taste. I eventually realized that the same is true of cigarette smoking as well. True, once people start smoking, often it becomes an addiction, but before the addiction—and even after—there is a pleasure factor involved, and that pleasure comes from the cigarette's taste. People who smoke love the taste, and they feel that taste in their mouths. In the same way that we put out Slim-Mint to help reduce people's taste acuity (which automatically reduces appetite) and thereby lose weight, we put out Ban-Smoke Gum to help reduce people's desire for cigarettes and thereby decrease smoking.

We brought out Ban-Smoke in 1960, well before the terrible health effects of smoking were widely known, and for a few years the product did not do very well. In fact, by 1964, many of our products were not doing well at all. Thompson Medical had over-expanded, and our product sales had actually declined. One weekend in January 1964, I was staying at Grossinger's Hotel in up-state New York, and I remember thinking that this is probably the last time I'll be able to get away to a hotel for a weekend, because business is terrible and the company's just about broke. Then, that Saturday night, I heard the Surgeon General announcing on the radio his report that cigarette smoking was dangerous, and that he wanted a warning on all cigarette packets cautioning people that smoking was dangerous to their health. I remember taking a deep breath, and thinking, "This is good. Maybe I'll sell more Ban-Smoke Gum, and it will pull me out of my economic decline."

That Monday, I came into the office and the phones just kept ringing off the hook. Very quickly, we sold out most of the stock we had. There is one order from that day that I still remember very clearly. It came from Revco, a drugstore chain based in Cleveland. Revco must have had fifty, maybe even a hundred stores. Their chief buyer was a fellow name Marvin Black, and he was tough. Until then, I had never been able to sell him any Slim-Mint or Ban-Smoke, and I had tried often. All of a sudden, he was on the phone, saying, "Danny, I want to buy twelve dozen Ban-Smoke Gum for every store." This was a huge order, 144 packages for every store in the Revco chain. I said to him, "Marvin, I can't in clear conscience sell you that much because you won't sell it." And he just repeated, "Danny, I want twelve dozen Ban-Smoke for each store." I tried again, "I'll sell it to you," I told him, "but I'm telling you now, I don't want to be on the receiving end of whatever you have to send back if you don't sell them and I can't guarantee that size sale to you." He answered with two words: "Ship it."

I sent out the order, he paid for it, and then about three months later, I got a call from him, "Danny, I want to return so many dozen Ban-Smoke Gum." I said to him, "Marvin, I told you at the time I could not guarantee the sale of such a big quantity, because it was too much per store." He paid no attention to what I was saying, "Well, I have to send it back, and you better send me a check." I told him that I didn't have the money to do so, but offered to ship him Slim-Mint Gum instead. He agreed and I was overjoyed. He returned the Ban-Smoke, I shipped him the Slim-Mint, and he pushed it aggressively, selling large quantities. Eventually we did millions of dollars of business with him with a whole variety of our products. We also became very good friends.

Part of what's important about this story is what happened at the beginning, and my philosophy of how to treat customers. I had really wanted to sell to Revco for a long time, but when Marvin Black finally called and wanted to make too large an order, I discouraged him. I never wanted to stick anyone with anything. I tried to make every experience with everyone I dealt with as pleasant as possible. I've always believed that the product remained ours until it reached the hands of a satisfied consumer. Until then, the retailer was just a middleman between us and the consumer. I wanted to keep the retailer happy, and I wanted to keep the consumer happy. Do that, and you'll end up with very happy results.

In any case, the Surgeon General's report really helped keep us in business. And we always—both before and after Ban-Smoke—kept bringing out other products as well. Figure-Aid was one, made up of vitamins, minerals, and Benzocaine. Another product was Aqua-Ban, a diuretic which helped eliminate excess water weight and swelling in the extremities. The product worked very effectively against water-bloat. A man named Richard Gayloff created wire-rack displays that could be pulled apart, and we used to put up large displays, titled Appetite Control Centers, in chain drugstores throughout the country. Those displays gave us the opportunity to showcase Slim-Mint, Ban-Smoke, Figure-Aid, and Aqua-Ban together. It was a great boon to sales.

One event that greatly fueled our growth in the world of weight loss was a new application of phenylpropanolamine (known as PPA). A buyer at Walgreens, one of our major customers, told me about a new product, X-11, that he was selling a ton of. It contained phenylpropanolamine, a product that had originally been introduced into the market years earlier as a nasal decongestant, and had now been found to work very effectively as an appetite suppressant. People were taking 25 milligrams three times a day. I learned that customers were coming back for the product again and again, and saying how much it was helping them lose weight. The fact that the same people were making repeat purchases is what impressed me. As I've said earlier, I was always conscious not to go into a product simply because someone else was selling a lot of it. People will buy something once. And since there are a lot of people out there, it can take a good while before you learn that the product might just be a fad. I never wanted to waste my time, and other people's money, on a fad, and the best proof that something is not a fad is if the same people come back for it again and again.

We checked into the product carefully, were impressed with what we learned, and soon came out with Appedrine, a quick-release, appetite suppressant to be taken three times a day, once before each meal. Later, we developed Prolamine, a time-released pill, which people could take twice a day in doses of 35 milligrams each. That way, people would be covered for lunch and dinner (most people didn't overeat, or certainly didn't overeat a lot, at breakfast). Eventually, this led us to Dexatrim, our most successful diet product prior to Slim-Fast. Once again, the product contained phenylpropanolamine, and it also contained caffeine as a stimulant. Like Prolamine, Dexatrim was time-released; at first we brought it out in 50 milligram doses, and later 75. It soon became the best-selling diet pill on the market, and helped Thompson Medical's sales surpass $50 million by the end of the seventies.

We had a fifth panel on the Dexatrim box (and on our other products as well), with messages such as "Lose weight and feel great," "Don't be fat" (a message, I learned, a lot of people didn't like), and "Lose weight! Reduce pounds and inches fast."

The fifth panel was actually an idea I had come up with years earlier and something I am very proud of. I described earlier the first advertising device I developed, the window sign, a small 1- or 2-inch newspaper ad blown up to an 8½-by-11-inch size, and then taped onto a drugstore window. These window signs were crucial to our early growth because we didn't have the money to advertise on radio or to take out large newspaper ads. Over the years, the window signs became bigger and more sophisticated. We started putting them out in two colors, and eventually we went from paper to thin, white cardboard signs. However, as drugstores modernized, they concluded that it would be better to clear off their windows so that customers could see directly into the store. It became harder and harder to find a place on the store windows to post our signs. I realized then that if we could no longer put the advertising message on the windows, we would have to find a way to put the message on the product itself. That was the beginning of the fifth panel idea. I decided to take a lip from the product, about 3 inches high, and put the same message on the lip that we used to put on the window signs. In the case of Slim-Mint Gum, we would print in bright, bold letters, "Lose Weight Fast," and in the case of San-Cura, "Stop Itch Fast." We were the first to develop this method of advertising. Even years later, I saw that other companies never understood how to properly use this fifth panel. The crucial thing, though, was to put the advertising message on that fifth panel. It helped our sales a lot.

I recently looked back at a company report from 1979, and was struck by the range and quantity of products we were producing:

—Bran-Slim Tablets, for weight control
—Quick Pep Tablets, for quick energy
—Caffedrine, time-released, to boost energy
—Vita-Hair, vitamins for the hair
—Aqua Ban, to eliminate excess water
—San-Cura, our first product, an anti-itch ointment
—Slim-Fast, our then recently developed liquid-meal-in-a-glass
—Balance, to balance calories and nutrition
—Aspercreme, an arthritis pain medication
—Slim-Line, a gum and candy used as an appetite suppressant
—Appedrine, Prolamine, and Dexatrim, our three most successful appetite suppressants
—Control, an additional, clinically proven appetite suppressant, which enabled people to control their appetite to slim down fast without going hungry
—Anorexin, a capsule for dieters promoted to doctors, which also worked as an appetitive suppressant
And finally,
—Coffee, Tea, and A New Me, also an appetite suppressant for weight loss.

I am proud of the care Thompson Medical took to develop products that were innovative, effective, and safe. In 1979, we had a total of eighteen M.D.s and Ph.D.s on our staff, headed by Dr. Ed Steinberg, my wonderful brother-in-law. The size and creativity of our staff enabled us to remain on the cutting edge of new product development, particularly in the area of weight control.

Hydrocortisone: From # 17 to # 1

When hydrocortisone, a powerful and effective anti-itch chemical, came on the market as an over-the-counter drug (until then, the product that people generally referred to as "cortisone" had required a prescription), all the drug companies rushed to market their own brands. Within a short time, there were sixteen brands on the market, and we were the seventeenth.* But how do you promote a brand when all your competitors are marketing essentially the same product?† What you really need in such a case is creativity, an approach that will make the consumer take immediate notice of your product. In the case of hydrocortisone, the first idea for how to catch consumers' attention was to name the product "Cortizone-5," a strong and attractive name, and to package the tube of ointment in a very attractive carton. Then came a blockbuster idea from Ed Horowitz, the buyer for Thrifty Drugs in California. This might sound odd at first that we got important advice for how to market a product from a buyer, but the truth is we got a lot of good ideas from our retail customers. We stayed on very good terms with the retailers, always listening to them

---

* It's common when a new product comes out for a lot of companies to enter the market. Then, slowly, as one company spends more on advertising and does better marketing, the others fall by the wayside.

† Not exactly the same. I am proud that our people at Thompson Medical Company developed a formula that pharmacists told us was the most effective of the cortisones on the market because of the product's ability to absorb into the skin.

so that we could give them what they needed. Listening to what customers want is at the heart of doing business successfully and doing it right. I used to say that a person is born with one mouth and two ears so that he should listen twice as much as he speaks. In any case, I am proud to say that our retail customers returned our friendship. I tell the story elsewhere of what a loyal friend Charlie Elson of Walgreens was, and how he would encourage me to bring out new products when he thought Thompson Medical Company had something special to offer, and how he would discourage me if he thought the product we were thinking of introducing had nothing in particular to recommend it (see pages 213-215). Anyway, Ed Horowitz said, "Danny, if you want to make a success of your Cortisone product, launch it with a Buy-One-Get-One-Free campaign." I asked him, "Do you mean I have to put two tubes in the package, or can I put in one tube with two ounces in it? That will be a lot easier to do." Ed said, "No, if you go with a Buy-One-Get-One-Free offer, you have to give the customers two tubes of one ounce each." It was, I realized, an expensive proposition, and it would also be difficult to put two tubes in one carton.

Quickly though, I decided to go along with Ed's idea. I realized that pharmacies weren't going to carry seventeen versions of the same product (they would want a maximum of two or three), and we therefore needed to come up with techniques that would make us stand out. But the Buy-One-Get-One-Free offer was only one part of the campaign we now developed. Another thing that set us off as different and memorable was, as noted, trademarking the name "Corti-zone" by using a "z" instead of an "s." We made one other change as well. When hydrocortisone was first taken off prescription, the FDA permitted companies to market only a half-percent strength. To consumers, a half of one percent doesn't sound all that impressive, yet all the other cortisones had the half-percent strength prominently listed on their packaging. Instead, we called our version, as noted, "Cortizone-5," the "5" being, in my view, much stronger. I remember sitting down at the time with my close friend Paul Craniotes, the Art Director for Thompson Medical Company. Paul was brilliant and very fast with a pad and art pencils. The two of us would talk about a product, spark each other, and he would be designing it as we talked. He had the ability to visualize what I was saying and put it on paper, which I couldn't do. And so, as we were dreaming up how we were going to compete in this market, Paul was already drafting the name Cortizone-5, and how the packaging could best be designed.

Finally, we also advertised on television, depicting a girl with a rash on her arm, as an announcer declared in the background, "Cortizone-5 stops the itch and heals the rashes fast." The camera then showed the girl rubbing on the ointment, and the rash quickly disappearing. The combination of these three things, the Buy-One-Get-One-Free offer, the name Cortizone-5, and the television ad, skyrocketed us from number seventeen to number one or two in the different national markets. A short time later, when the FDA permitted a one percent ointment to be released, we put out Cortizone-10, which instantly did very well. In 1996, we sold the product to Pfizer for almost a $100 million, a pretty remarkable result for a product that had started out in seventeenth place.

One final thought about business, and this applies to any business you're in, and should apply in your personal life as well. Every year, whether sales were up or down—and there were years when they were down by more than half—we always made a profit. There was no magic to that. It was simply this: As soon as sales started to fall, we would cut expenses quickly and, when we needed to, we would cut deeply. Part of the reason we were able to do so was that *I never had a budget.* I know that sounds odd, but I think things can work out much better that way. Not having a budget caused us to manage all our business affairs day by day. When sales were up, we could quickly increase our expenditures, especially in advertising (I always tried to push a winner). When sales were down, the lack of a formal budget gave us the flexibility to reduce expenses very quickly. I think this strategy works for companies, and it will work in your personal life as well.

VI

Slim-Fast: The Beginning

In 1976, a national craze was developing in America, beginning with what were called, in those days, "protein-sparing fasting diets." The idea was to create a diet in which people ate no solid food at all; all they would consume were liquids—essentially water—along with a protein mix. In the first diet of this kind that swept the country, the dieter would supplement his fast with four tablespoons of something called collagen, a red-colored protein that was extracted from the skin of dead cows. The product's promoters claimed that the extraction was 100 percent pure protein. Although I myself never tried the mix, the reports I consistently heard were that the taste was terrible but the results fantastic, and that people were losing tremendous amounts of weight. This, of course, made sense. Anyone will lose weight, and lose it quickly, on a very low-calorie diet. Stories were published of people invited to state dinners at the White House who wouldn't partake of any food. Instead, they brought along their collagen, and then mixed it with water.

Some medical professionals expressed concern that such a diet could generate health problems, especially since some dieters were adhering to this regimen for three or four months at a time. The collagen advocates pooh-poohed such fears, claiming that the very purity of the protein liquid would protect dieters from the effects of a prolonged fast. This was later proven to be false.

While the notion of ingesting no solid food whatsoever seemed wrong to me from the get-go, what struck me with even greater force was what the quick success of this product revealed. Overweight people did not want a complicated diet. They wanted a simple way to lose weight, one that wouldn't require them to make constant decisions: "Can I eat this food? If so, how much can I have? Do I need to go around with a miniature scale, and weigh everything I put into my mouth?" Eliminating such questions and concerns made a complete liquid diet, accompanied by a few spoonfuls of protein, so attractive. It took away the temptation created by having solid food on the table. Because the moment you allow any solid foods as part of the dieting regimen, the temptation, especially for heavy people, will be to continue eating.

But I also sensed that simply giving people protein, and nothing else, was not sufficient, either. What I wanted to bring to market, therefore, was a meal replacement in liquid form, composed of protein, carbohydrates, vitamins, and minerals, and even a little healthy fat. My idea was to mix all these things into a powder, blend it with skim milk, and then you'd have a nutritious meal in a glass. That's why I made sure that Slim-Fast had, from the beginning, all the essential vitamins and minerals.

Also, I couldn't see offering Slim-Fast as a *total* replacement for solid foods. I kept thinking that there was something fundamentally unhealthy about doing that. It also goes against human nature. How many people would be able to stick to an exclusively liquid diet for more than a few days? Who knows how many people were cheating on their pure liquid diet? I didn't know the answer to that question, but I suspected that there were a lot of them. It's common knowledge that many people don't adhere strictly to diets. So when we first marketed Slim-Fast, we advocated having it for breakfast, lunch, and a snack, followed by a sensible dinner. That way, between the three daily glasses and then the dinner, you would be consuming no more than about 1,500 calories a day, and would lose weight—without ever going hungry.

That's how we first started Slim-Fast, in 1977—as a powder mixed with skim milk. I came up with the name, together with our art director, a man named Paul Craniotes, who was also one of my best friends. We wanted to convey a few things in the product's name, most importantly, that if you follow this diet, you'll get slim quickly. Also, that it's a form of a fast—you'll be kept away the whole day, until dinnertime, from the temptation of consuming solid food—so that people could immediately understand why Slim-Fast was innovative and would work.

People sometimes ask me if I realized right away that Slim-Fast had the potential to become my biggest product. The truth is—though people are always surprised when I say this—I never thought about that. I've always had a pretty simple personal philosophy about work. You take everything one day at a time, and make sure to do all that you can during that day. You use the full range of your ingenuity to promote a good idea. And enjoy yourself! Never underestimate the enjoyment factor, which, unfortunately, too many people do. They take their work—and themselves—too seriously, worrying so much about the possibility of making an error that they lose the ability to take pleasure on a daily basis from what they are doing. I was certainly committed to working hard, but I always enjoyed what I was doing.

Growing up, I never thought about becoming rich. In fact, my earliest recollection of a rich man was unattractive. During the summer, I used to go to the beach every day in Long Beach. In the summer, my dad and mom would often go to the beach in the early morning and take a swim, and on those long summer days, businessmen would come home on the train from New York City and stroll along the beach while it was still light. I was a young kid, maybe ten or eleven at the time, and I remember seeing one very wealthy man— at least that was the reputation he had. I don't know how much money he really had. In those days of the Depression, it sometimes seemed as if anybody who could pay his bills was wealthy. The word was that this man was really rich. But he was also very out of shape, and it was clear that he made very little effort to take care of himself. When I saw him take off his robe to go into the ocean, I remember thinking: *True, it's very im-*

portant to earn a good living, but it's also very important to keep yourself fit.

Anyway, to get back to Slim-Fast. One of the things I'm compulsive about is continuing to work on a product, even after it's on the market. Say your product is the best one out there when you first bring it out. It won't remain the best if you don't keep improving it; sooner or later—usually sooner—someone will come up with something better.

In this regard, I must own up to something about myself. No matter how well a business is going, I always feel somewhat insecure about it. I know in my heart that sales could fall to zero quickly. That's true for every product and every company. Look at the decline in recent years in General Motors. When I was growing up, GM was the model of a stable and highly successful company; for many years it was the most profitable corporation in the United States. (There was even a popular saying back in the mid-twentieth century: "What's good for General Motors is good for the country.") In those days, had someone predicted that competition from the Japanese and other foreign automakers would drive GM to its knees, force it to lay off tens of thousands of workers, and file for bankruptcy, that would have sounded preposterous. But General Motors didn't keep producing better cars at good prices, while its competitors did. So the company declined. Numerous large corporations have fared even worse than General Motors, disappearing altogether.

I have always believed that the time to be nervous is not when your product starts failing in the market; by then it might well be too late. The time to start worry-

ing about your product is when you're at the height of
your success. You can be sure that there are plenty of
competitors looking at how to improve on your product
and give you some tough competition. So why wait for
them to figure out how to make your product better?
Improve it yourself first, and continuously, so that your
customers will continue to use your product because
it's the best. Ultimately, the more satisfaction consumers get—the more loyal they are going to be.

That's how it came about that a short time after
Slim-Fast came to market, my brother-in-law and business associate Dr. Eddie Steinberg* and I heard about

---

* Eddie was now full-time medical director at Thompson Medical.
Around 1976, it became clear to me that the FDA, empowered by
Congress, was going to investigate all medical products produced in
the United States. I realized that we didn't have sufficient scientific
support for the claims we were making for our weight-loss product
Dexatrim, which was our most successful product at the time. I
called up Eddie, who was then practicing optometry in New York
City and in Long Beach. I said to him, "I have a big favor to ask of
you. Give up your practice, and your association with the Eye Clinic
at Hillsdale Hospital, and start a research arm for Thompson Medical to develop clinical studies to support our claims for the efficacy
and safety of Dexatrim." Eddie had a very successful career—an article he had published about Abraham Lincoln's eye problems had
just been reported on in the *New York Times*—but loyal and good
brother-in-law that he was, he agreed to help me. By the time the
FDA sent us a letter telling us that we would be evaluated and in-
vestigated, he had developed a group of prominent physicians who
had already initiated clinical studies to support our claims. When
we had to appear before the FDA—we came with heads of medical
departments throughout the United States and Europe—we were
able to demonstrate unequivocally that our products were both safe
and effective. Eddie did an excellent job. We got the approval we
needed from the FDA, and, subsequently, the profits generated by
Dexatrim enabled us to develop, promote, and expand Slim-Fast.

a physician doing important work at Harvard Medical School, Dr. George Blackburn, a professor of nutrition, and both an MD and a PhD. We got in touch with George and he agreed to see us "after work." Well after work. We ended up coming to his apartment at about 11 p.m. George soon became a best friend and has remained so ever since. What Eddie and I were quizzing him about at that first meeting was what he thought, as a nutritionist, it would take to provide a healthy, low-calorie meal for people trying to lose weight. At the time, there were people putting themselves on 800-calorie-a-day liquid diets under a physician's supervision, and we wanted to create something as healthy, if not healthier, that would not rely on constant medical supervision, could be sold inexpensively over the counter, and could be used safely by anyone seeking to lose weight. George offered us wonderful advice that night—and throughout the years, until we sold Slim-Fast in 2000. He remained the best repository of advice on how to maintain a high level of nutrition in Slim-Fast. He also provided us with a good definition of what Slim-Fast was, one that conveyed—to the FDA and all other interested parties—why it was safe and needed no medical supervision: "The product is made from milk, fortified with vitamins, minerals, and fiber, and contains no appetite suppressants or any weight-loss drug. It is obviously a food, a meal replacement, and falls within the category established by the United States Food and Drug Administration, 'food for special dietary purposes.'"

George's advice was just the sort of input I was looking for. I was very concerned about making sure that we had the right amount of each vitamin, mineral, and protein, along with enough fiber and calcium. But it wasn't just nutrition I was concerned about. I was also very concerned about taste—and price. I always believed that it was my responsibility to make sure that consumers always had the best possible product— which meant not just healthy, but best-tasting as well—at the lowest possible price. In short, the product had to taste good, be inexpensive, and help consumers lost weight. I spent a lot of time working on making the nutrition better and better. I knew that consumers wouldn't know the difference, and most of them didn't care as long as it was at a level that could be called healthy or well-balanced. But I needed to know that it was as nutritious as it could be, because I couldn't sell anything I didn't believe was the best. In my view, if you don't believe in what you're selling, you can't sell it effectively. Certainly not for long.

Slim-Fast caught on quickly. People were buying large quantities of the powder, mixing it with skim milk, and losing weight. We kept tinkering with the formula to make it tastier, and we succeeded. It was delicious.

Even so, the diet business went through some rough times (just to give you an idea, the first year we did $600,000 in sales, the next year $100,000). A year after we started marketing the Slim-Fast powder, liquid protein collagen was implicated in the deaths of about fifty people. The government never took the product off the market, however, because it wasn't the product itself that was harming dieters. It was the lack of potassium in their diet. A potassium deficiency can cause the heart to go into a sudden fibrillation, and give out. That was one part of the problem. Then there were people who would go on this total liquid fast for months at a time (very few people had the willpower to actually do that), and then decide to break the fast at a wedding or some other kind of celebration. The intake of large quantities of food after months of essentially fasting would cause the body to go into shock. But even though liquid protein collagen was never formally banned, the government announcement that the protein-sparing fasting diet had caused the death of some fifty people prompted sales of all diet products to plummet.

But we stayed with it. What we had been emphasizing since the beginning was that Slim-Fast should not be a total diet. Our refrain had long been: "Two shakes a day and a sensible dinner."

Gradually, Slim-Fast's sales built back up again. And, strangely enough, one of the things that helped that happen was a competitor. People often assume that competition must be bad for business. But that's not always the case. In 1980, just a few years after we'd started marketing Slim-Fast, the Cambridge Diet—which, as its name suggests, came from England—was introduced into the United States and took the market by storm. The Cambridge Diet was a powder, very much like Slim-Fast, but it was sold house to house. That made the product's markup enormous. It was being sold for something like $24 a can, while we were selling Slim-Fast for $6 for a comparable quantity. But the truth is, the Cambridge Diet was generating enormous sales. One of the things it had going for it was its name. People associate "Cambridge" with one of the finest universities in the world, and assume that a product with that name must be of very high quality. But I also knew that Slim-Fast contained more protein, tasted better, and sold for a quarter of the price. Therefore, we decided to compete directly against the Cambridge Diet, and took out ads focusing on Slim-Fast's great advantages. After emphasizing our increased protein, our great taste, and our lower price, our clincher was, "The Cambridge Diet or Slim-Fast? For fast, easy weight loss, the choice is clear."

I thought that headline was pretty good, and it brought Slim-Fast roaring back. I was always very involved in our advertising campaigns. I had spent my teenage years publishing the *Long Island Beacon*, honing my writing skills, and there is nothing like writing headlines to really force you to get to the essence of the message you want to convey. Like, "Wake up, America . . ." Or "The Cambridge Diet or Slim-Fast? . . . the choice is clear."

During those early years of competition with the Cambridge Diet, our sales increased from $20 million to $40 million and then to $80 million. Eventually, the worst thing that happened to us is that the Cambridge Diet started to fade from the scene. This was a blow to our advertising, since we now had nothing to compare Slim-Fast to. Our sales, which had gone up so quickly, now started to fall, not as dramatically as they had risen, but still very substantially. It was a difficult, sometimes traumatic period.

Sales gradually picked up again when we initiated an advertising campaign using consumer testimonials ("I lost seven pounds in seven days with Slim-Fast," "I lost ten pounds in ten days"). This campaign was developed by my niece Deborah Steinberg with Ronnie Stern, the company's president and my cousin's son, and my daughter Tammy. Still, I was frustrated. By the late 1980s, it was clear to me that with all the people in the country who wanted to lose weight, we were hitting only a small percentage of the market. How could we get more? And then one day in 1988, Oprah Winfrey went on her television show wearing a coat, and opened it to reveal that she had lost sixty-seven pounds on a product called Optifast. Optifast was, like Slim-Fast, a powder-based diet, and quite similar in composition. Unlike Slim-Fast, however, it couldn't be bought over the counter. It was a hospital-based meal-replacement program and the only way you could get it was under a doctor's supervision at a hospital. In the aftermath of Oprah's revelation, viewers, desperate to rid themselves of unwanted pounds, descended on pharmacies all over the United States. The pharmacists explained that they could not sell them Optifast, but told them that a very similar product, Slim-Fast, required no prescription and could achieve similar results. The effect on our sales was dramatic, and even though Oprah's experience was wonderful advertising for Optifast, it equally, and unintentionally, benefited us.

I now saw even greater potential for Slim-Fast than I had before. The country had gone wild after the Oprah show, and it soon occurred to me what we needed to do to propel Slim-Fast's sales exponentially.

VII

Celebrity Endorsements and Why They Matter: It's Not What You Think

It was late winter 1988, and I was sitting in my office with my lovely daughter Tammy, Slim-Fast's president Ronnie Stern, and Jeff Stein, our account executive at Grey Advertising. We were discussing, as we had already done several times, the recent and amazing upsurge in sales both for Optifast and Slim-Fast. What we were trying to figure out was why the excitement generated by Oprah's weight loss was so great. Why the huge response to Oprah's double-digit weight loss and the tremendous increase in sales of weight-loss products? Was it only because she was a celebrity? The answer was yes but, it seemed to me, not for the reason most of us think. We assume that because people know and admire Oprah they cared so much more about her weight loss. But that, I believe, is only part of the reason. When an attractive but unknown Joan Smith, for example, appears in a bathing suit on television, announces that she's lost seventy-five pounds, and holds up earlier highly unattractive photos of herself, people are not convinced in their gut. Because the viewers never knew Joan Smith in her overweight years, it's hard for them to accept that they could ever end up looking the way she does now. But because Oprah was so much in the public eye, people knew in their heads that everything she was saying was true. They didn't have to imagine what she looked like before she lost sixty pounds. They knew, because they saw her all the time. So when she took off her coat and announced her weight loss, they believed her. In addition, Oprah was an actress, so her enthusiasm about her diet and its results was contagious.

At some point during the meeting, I remember saying, "Why don't we get a celebrity who everybody knows needs to lose weight, put her on a Slim-Fast diet, and if she loses weight successfully, we can shoot commercials with her. And there's no reason we shouldn't get the same incredible results."

So Jeff said, "I think we should go after Tommy Lasorda."

To which I responded, "Who's Tommy Lasorda?" At this point in my life, I was not following sports closely at all.

I was quickly informed that Tommy Lasorda was the most famous manager in baseball, and that people all over the country were very aware of who he was. Lasorda was also famously overweight, a condition that had recently caused his Los Angeles Dodgers players to offer to donate $20,000 to the charity of his choice if he could take off twenty pounds by the midseason All-Star game. The offer, I learned, had gotten a lot of publicity.

One thought, though, worried me: Will Lasorda sell to women? Weight loss at that time was overwhelmingly a women's business. We had long estimated that 80 to 90 percent of diet sales were to women. By the way, that's no longer true, and I'm proud to claim that the way we promoted and advertised Slim-Fast influenced a lot more men to actively lose weight.

It did not take long for Jeff, Ronnie, and Tammy to convince me that we should speak to Lasorda. In my normal, direct manner, I said, "Let's call him right now."

"No, no, no," they answered, almost in unison. "That's not the way things work. You have to go through someone."

Maybe, but I've always known that things happen a lot more quickly when you don't go through someone, but rather go directly to the person at the top, the one who can make the decision. Which meant Lasorda.

It was March, and the Dodgers were in spring training in Vero Beach, Florida. By now, it was the early evening, and I don't recall exactly how we did it, but a few minutes later, Lasorda was picking up the phone. "Tommy," I said to him. "This is Dan Abraham from Slim-Fast. I heard that your players gave you an offer to lose twenty pounds by the All-Star break. Why don't you use Slim-Fast, lose the weight, and we'll shoot you in commercials while you're doing it?"

I had never met Lasorda—indeed, until a few minutes earlier, I had never even heard of him—but he was a pretty tough character, with a gruff manner. I later concluded that his signature gruffness was part of his charm. Anyway, he rebuffed me right off the bat. "Everyone's been calling me since that player challenge—Weight Watchers, this one, that one. But I'm not going on any of that junk."

The last thing in the world I needed was for Lasorda to suddenly clank down the phone and end all chances of a deal. "Tommy," I said, "let me come down and show you Slim-Fast, and I'll give you a $20,000 check made out to your favorite charity. That's what your players offered you to lose twenty pounds, but I'll give it to you just for spending a few minutes hearing our story."

This caught his attention. "Okay, come down at midnight." And then he did slam down the phone.

I looked around the room from face to face. "How the hell are we going to get down from Manhattan to Vero Beach by midnight?" It must have been six by then.

Jeff was the only one in the room who had had experience working at a company that occasionally chartered planes, and he knew how to do it. He said, "Why don't we charter a plane and get down there?"

It was the first time for all of us—except Jeff—flying on a private plane. And it worked out just as planned. A few minutes before midnight, we arrived at the Dodgers' training camp, carrying our Slim-Fast powder, a blender, cold milk, and ice—plus our check for $20,000. I was walking toward Lasorda's cabin, while he was walking toward us from his daughter's cabin. I took one look at him and I panicked. I remember exactly what went through my mind: "If I ever saw a heart attack candidate walking toward me, that's him." And my next thought was, *How in hell can we put him on Slim-Fast? This guy will have a heart attack, and people will say it was Slim-Fast that caused it.*

But we were down there, and we were going to meet with him. So I just forced myself to calm down. *Don't jump to conclusions. If it works out, we'll send him to a doctor and have him examined.*

Meanwhile, we all stepped into Lasorda's cabin and, in his trademark style, he greeted us: "All right, let me see your junk." I slowed things down a bit, and told him the Slim-Fast story, and how it's a complete meal in a glass. And then we mixed it up. He tasted it, and said, "Hey, it's not bad," which I realized by then was a high compliment coming from him.

If I was going to push, now was the time. I said to him. "Tommy, if you go on the Slim-Fast diet, lose twenty pounds by the All-Star break, we will then be able to advertise that in commercials that might pay you up to a million dollars." All we would want, I explained, was for him to have one Slim-Fast shake for breakfast, a second for lunch, a third at some point for a snack, and a sensible dinner.

As soon as he said, "Okay"—a million dollars is not an insignificant amount of money—I told him he needed to be examined by a doctor. I was still nervous about how overweight he looked. Fortunately, within a few days the Dodgers were in Los Angeles, and my dear friend Dr. George Blackburn arranged for Tommy to be examined by Dr. David Heber, a great physician and a professor of clinical nutrition at UCLA Medical School. Heber gave Lasorda a complete physical, and told us he was in good enough shape to go on the Slim-Fast diet.

Lasorda loved food, but he was well-motivated, and we monitored him carefully. We checked up on him constantly (weighing him daily) and, over the coming months, it was clear the weight was coming off. By the time the All-Star break arrived, he had more than fulfilled his side of the deal. I remember very clearly that first commercial we shot with him. I worked on it closely with my daughter Tammy, who has a really good eye and instinct for putting commercials together. And I think I'm pretty effective at wordsmithing ads. Lasorda stood in front of the camera and said, "Hi. I'm Tommy Lasorda. My teammates challenged me to lose twenty pounds by the All-Star break. . . . Well, I lost thirty pounds in three months on the Ultra Slim-Fast plan and it was easy. A shake for breakfast, a shake for lunch, and a sensible dinner—even pasta." And then the killer ending—I still remember it word for word: "If I can do it, *you* can do it!"

I've been in business for well over fifty years, and I've never experienced anything like what happened over the following weeks. Sales skyrocketed. Overnight, we went from doing a $100 million a year in sales to $300 million. Nonstop demands were coming in: "Ship the order! Ship the order!" We found ourselves going to factories all over the country, just to find new places to make Slim-Fast.

Lasorda became our best spokesperson and we also became very friendly. We organized many dinners for him in New York at his favorite restaurants. Twelve people at a dinner, and there were always many more who wanted to come. Over the years we arranged many publicity events for him. The one condition we made was that he had to maintain his weight loss to remain our spokesperson. And even though he loved to eat, he always kept the weight off.

The whole Lasorda experience reminded me yet again—as if I needed a reminder—that business, when done right, is such an amazingly thrilling adventure.

TAKING A RISK AND BETTING ON IT HEAVILY

There was another pivotal moment in Slim-Fast's growth. As was the case with Lasorda, it also tied in with advertising and, strangely enough, with America's first war in Iraq, the war that was generally referred to as Operation Desert Storm. At the time, America's president was George H. W. Bush. The United States was leading the attack against Iraq because of its illegal occupation of Kuwait. The war began in January 1991, with extensive bombing of Iraq. In fact, Operation Desert Storm consisted in the beginning of just air operations. The idea was not to send in ground troops until the areas they would be going into were safe, or at least as safe as possible. At the time—I don't even remember how it came about—I met the president of one of the TV networks.

I asked the network president how we could buy TV time more effectively. You see, payment for advertising was based on "cost per thousand exposures," and every program was monitored by a rating service so that networks and advertisers knew how many people were watching every hour on every show. At that time, our advertising was not show-specific. We didn't care what program was on when we advertised; we just wanted to make sure we were reaching a lot of people. But we also wanted to find out if there was a way we could reach even more people without greatly increasing our advertising costs. The network president said, "Look, in a few days the land war in Iraq is going to start"—we all knew that the bombing was intended to soften up the enemy for the ground invasion—"and when the land war starts every national advertiser has told us that they'll be canceling their advertising, especially during prime-time programming." This was important to know because prime-time television is normally far and away the most expensive time slot in which to advertise. He explained to me that companies were afraid to be running ads at a time when the news programs would likely be showing American troops in body bags. It turned out that the presidents of the companies doing the advertising all assumed that there were going to be large-scale American deaths as soon as the land war began, and that the networks would be doing continuous war coverage. There was no way these companies wanted their products associated with such unhappy images. That's when he made his offer to me: If I were willing to make a commitment to buy time on television after the land war, I could have it at an 80 to 90 percent discount, and that included prime-time television, a segment we had always avoided because it was so expensive. I immediately told him he had a deal: We would commit to between two and four ads an hour during the three prime-time hours.*

Even at reduced rates, this was a lot of money. I was willing to do it because I had fought in World War II,

---

* I later learned that the networks referred to our deal as the "airplane deal" because they could land our spots any time they wanted to within the shows.

and I knew from personal experience about the terrible effects of bombing on enemy soldiers. I understood that our air force was already in there decimating the Iraqi ground forces; not just punishing them physically, but psychologically as well. Even if you survive bombings day after day, you're certainly not in the mood to fight. All you want to do is get the hell out of there. Of one thing I was certain: After this level of bombing and destruction, when American troops went in, the other side wasn't going to come out with their weapons blazing, but with their arms up in surrender.

During the long bombing campaign, the Iraqi troops had no one to whom they could surrender. And if the Iraqi soldiers tried to run off into the desert, their commanders would shoot them in the back. That's why I felt so confident (even though it would normally be hard for me to make such a large financial commitment), and was willing to jump at the chance to buy all this airtime. It wasn't, of course, that I was insensitive to people who were dying—it was just that I thought they weren't going to die at all.

What I had predicted came to pass. There were almost no body bags. And it was during this intense period of advertising, carried on during prime-time television night after night, that Slim-Fast became even more widely known, and our sales once again increased tremendously.

VIII

Slim-Fast and the Philosophy of Continuous Improvement

The great increase in sales that started with the Lasorda period served us well for a good while, until we decided that there was another big market out there that we were missing: the people who wanted an easy diet, but who felt that it was too time-consuming and inconvenient to have to measure powder and mix it with milk. The reason America is a fast-food culture is because ours is an impatient culture. When television first began, you'd flick on the set and it would take maybe fifteen or twenty seconds until the picture and sound appeared. People didn't like that, so they developed television sets that turned on in an instant. The same with powdered diets. Many people were willing to mix the powder, but we suspected that there were far more who were not. And even though the powder was cheaper, we knew that if we brought out Slim-Fast in ready-to-drink form like a can of soda, there would be a whole new—and larger—market of people who would use it.

Unfortunately, for a long time, it was very difficult to get Slim-Fast in a can to taste good. That's because when you put a liquid product containing milk on the shelf without refrigeration, you need to subject it to excessive heat in order to pasteurize it. Unfortunately, that heating is hell on the taste. That's why a bottle or carton of fresh, refrigerated chocolate milk tastes so much better than a can of chocolate milk.

And that is precisely why, when we launched Slim-Fast as a prepared drink in late 1989, I was actually against it, and had to be argued into it. I didn't feel it tasted good enough, but the other guys in the company would say to me, "Danny, come on. People want it. It doesn't taste that bad." And I said, "Yes, it does." And they kept telling me, "No, it doesn't. And we need to come out with it now."

In any case, I didn't feel we had developed the taste of liquid Slim-Fast to the level that I wanted. It certainly didn't taste nearly as good as the powdered drink, and I didn't want to release it. But our sales force kept pressing me: "Danny, you've got to come out with this because if you don't, someone else will come out with something like it and beat us to the punch." It reminded me of my early days when my pharmacist friends kept telling me I needed to come out with a product to compete with Special Formula Gum (see page 80). Anyway, when you have a company, there are times you have to listen to the people who work there and who are as dedicated to its success as you are, even if they disagree with you. This is one time I did that.

But I couldn't pretend that everything was all right. I was also relying on a program we always had in the company, a process called "continuous improvement" (something I try to incorporate into my personal life as well). No matter how successful a product is, we keep working to improve it. So with all my skepticism, I knew that in time we would reach the goal of a great-tasting product. And I knew how important that was. We used to say that when it comes to anything we put in a consumer's mouth, "Taste is king, price is queen."

In the meantime, though, I did fear that we would disappoint some of our customers. So, as we did with all our products, we included a money-back guarantee with it. If you're not satisfied with anything, just return the product to the store and you'll get a full refund.

A few people did bring back their cans, but very few. Even though our first liquid Slim-Fast didn't taste as good as it should have, people were so pleased at the convenience of just opening a tab and having, without any preparation, a nutritious meal-in-a-drink that they were willing to sacrifice some taste.

Nonetheless, we did hear some complaints from consumers who argued that there were inconsistencies in taste, that a can bought, let's say, in Portland, Oregon, tasted different, and maybe inferior, to one purchased in Philadelphia. It seemed bizarre, because our production plans were identical all over the country. So I asked my brother-in-law and dear friend Dr. Ed Steinberg to check into this and find out if there was any basis to the complaints. It turned out that there was, and the solution to this problem ended up turning Slim-Fast into a better product and a better company.

You see, when we started marketing Slim-Fast in a can, we were producing it at six different facilities throughout the United States. And while the formulation of the drink was identical in each facility, the quality of the water differed from one place to another, as did the quality of the workers in the different plants. What Eddie concluded was that we needed one major manufacturing facility in one place; this would guarantee the uniformity of the product and its taste. Working with the help of CFO Carl T. Tsang and engineer Martin Sears, Eddie spent several years on this project, and we ended up with an extraordinarily efficient and consistent facility in Covington, Tennessee. Eddie had retained a consulting firm that did a detailed geographical analysis and selected Covington, which is near Memphis. Years later, I felt that having this kind of efficient production facility was a positive influence on the people from Unilever when they looked into the desirability of purchasing the company.

In any case, at first, our advertising just focused on liquid Slim-Fast's convenience, nutritional benefits, and weight-loss benefits. There was no mention of taste. But the efforts of the people in "continuous improvement" soon paid off. They kept working with our suppliers and development people on the product's taste. Every week, I was being brought new batches of product that were developed in the laboratory, and the taste really was improving. It was, as I learned, not so much an issue of putting in new ingredients, but other factors that I would not have anticipated. Particularly important was the sequence in which the ingredients were added. For example, do you first put in powdered milk mixed with water, or fresh milk? At what point do you insert the vitamins into the formula? We also had to decide which flavors to use, because there was such a variety of them. All this work paid off, and within months, the drink tasted delicious. A short time later, this comprehensive effort saved us from what might have been a disaster.

On the West Coast, Nestlé was test-marketing a weight-loss drink called Sweet Success. The name was attractive and the product tasted very good. In those areas in which Nestlé was trying out the drink, they were gaining up to a 50 percent market share. Nestlé kept emphasizing the product's taste. People who need to lose weight are often the very people who are most seduced by good taste. But we quickly pre-empted them with a national advertising campaign focusing on how good Slim-Fast tasted, and despite Sweet Success's early success, it never developed into a national product.

Meanwhile, Dr. George Blackburn kept his focus on balancing the right amount of vitamins, calcium, protein, and fiber in the product. We relied on George to make sure that Slim-Fast was the best product possible for the purpose for which we were selling it—meal replacement. I was then, and still remain, very proud of what we created. I used to think that if we could bring this drink out in a chocolate bar, with the same mix of protein, vitamins, minerals, fiber, and calcium, its balance of energy and nutrition would have made a far healthier meal for the army to give out to soldiers than what I used to get during my World War II days (hard chocolate bars that were almost impossible to chew).

Thomas Medical products and especially Slim-Fast had long been moving along almost with a momentum of their own, and in 1990 we had taken the company private. We continued to advertise the product heavily, but what was enormously helpful was word of mouth. Millions of people were using Slim-Fast, losing substantial amounts of weight, and telling their friends. These friends, who witnessed the weight loss, were impressed, and this, of course, was the best advertising of all.

Sales were now growing 20 percent annually. It was exciting to me as I traveled, both around the country and around the world, to go into stores and see this product—which only a few years earlier had simply been an idea in my head—prominently displayed, and helping people to lose weight.

Just as an aside, it has often occurred to me that I wish we had a better expression for becoming slimmer than *to lose weight*. The word "lose" has such negative connotations. Who, after all, wants to be a *loser*? In no other area of life does anyone want to be considered a loser. We all want to be winners. I am convinced that we need to come up with a more positive and upbeat-sounding expression to associate with weight reduction;* otherwise, the negative association with the word "lose" will unconsciously keep some people off diets. For that matter, the word "diet" also is pejorative, inasmuch as it implies something temporary, rather than a lifestyle change.

---

* For example, rather than focusing on the loss of weight, we should focus on how, by cutting down on what you eat, you're gaining control of your life, your health, and general feeling of well-being.

Anyway, sales and profits were now rising substantially year to year. By 2000, we were doing about $650 million in sales and bringing in a pretax profit of about $120 million. With the bullish economic climate prevailing in America (due, in large part, to the very successful presidency of a man I admire greatly and whom I proudly regard as a friend, Bill Clinton), it made sense to consider the possibility of selling Slim-Fast. I was moving into my late seventies, and in addition to business, my involvement in trying to help bring about peace to the Middle East was growing.

Together with a few of my top people, I went to Goldman Sachs and told their representatives that we'd like to try to sell the company. The people who worked with us at Goldman Sachs were very professional in their approach to the sale. They arranged with us to do what's called a "dog-and-pony show," in which you meet with potential purchasers and get them excited about your company. We put together a book outlining all the financial details, and the history and profile of Slim-Fast. The Goldman Sachs people sent it around to companies whom they had reason to believe might be interested in it; this was a time when big companies were acquiring brands. Unilever was one of those that came to look at our company, and we made a big presentation to its people. The top guy from Unilever who came out that day was someone I was told to look out for and to make feel comfortable. I went over to him and introduced myself, but even as I was extending my hand, he shot past me; it was clear that he did not want to spend any time in conversation. It was also clear, though, that he was paying close attention to the many presentations made by our top people. He listened carefully to all of them—the people from sales, marketing, advertising, and manufacturing. In addition, I could see him paying particular attention to the scientific discussion of Slim-Fast, how it worked and the science behind it. Then, at the end of the presentations, we offered drinks of Slim-Fast at the back of the room. Strangely enough, the other people from Unilever weren't going over to taste it; most likely, they already had. But this guy did walk to the back, and I went over to him and told him about the various flavors in which Slim-Fast was available. He picked up two different cans, opened one, and took a sip. I still remember the look of surprise on his face when he realized that it tasted good. Just like the response years earlier, when Tommy Lasorda tasted Slim-Fast and said, "It's not bad." As I looked at this man now, drinking Slim-Fast and enjoying it, I got excited. OK, I thought to myself, now he's really interested.

In truth, though I'm a people person, I never got overly friendly with this fellow. He did become warmer later, after he made his bid, and some years later, when he changed jobs, he called me up to discuss some business idea. What I realized was that he was a nice guy, but he didn't want to get friendly with Slim-Fast's chief salesman—me—and possibly be unduly influenced by our relationship. He wanted all his decisions to be strictly business.

When the meeting ended, it seemed clear that there was interest on Unilever's part, but I still had no idea if a deal was going to be struck. A few weeks later I was on my boat, *Netanya V*, with George Blackburn.

We were docked in the Caribbean, when a call came through late Friday afternoon. The Goldman Sachs executive said to me, "Danny, are you sitting down?"

I said, "Yeah, why? Did they walk away?'

He said, "No."

"Did a new company come in?"

"No."

"So why should I be sitting down?"

He said, "Unilever gave us a preemptive bid."

I said, "What is that?" and he explained that Unilever was ready to buy the company right now, and not have it offered to anyone else.

"Okay," I said, "but I still don't know why I should be sitting down."

"Because they bid $2.3 billion." While I was absorbing this astronomical figure, he asked, "Should I ask him for more?"

"No," I said, very decisively. "Just lock the door and don't let him out until we close the deal."

In light of all that was happening I was, I thought, pretty calm. Nonetheless, when I got off the phone I asked George to take my pulse. It was over 90. Normally my sitting pulse is 55.

I had come a long way from the boy who panicked over what to do when he broke a two-cent bottle of milk while walking to the grocery store in Long Beach.

IX

My Life in Israel: Seven Remarkable Years

I grew up in a passionately Zionist household, and that passion only grew as I got older. In the early years after World War II, I became a charter member of the Zionist Organization of America (ZOA). I can still recall the pro-statehood rallies we, along with other Zionist groups, organized in the months after the United Nations voted to partition Palestine into a Jewish and an Arab state (November 29, 1947). Then, in May 1948, Israel was created. In the following years, I remained a very passionate and committed advocate for Israel, but because of the expense involved and later my work pressures, I didn't get a chance to visit Israel during the first twenty years of its existence.

Many years later, in the late 1960s, at a pro-Israel fund-raiser at our synagogue, I was asked to contribute $10,000 to the United Jewish Appeal (UJA). That was a very large sum of money for me then, and over the coming year I was not able to pay off my pledge. Then, a year later, the UJA people asked me to renew my pledge. I told them no, that I hadn't paid off the last pledge and therefore couldn't undertake another $10,000. They told me, "Don't worry, we trust you. Besides, if you pledge the money, you'll help lead the way, inspire others, and eventually you'll pay off your own pledges, too." So I renewed my pledge, and they were right. It did help inspire others, and eventually I paid off both pledges.

Today, trying to forge peace between Israel and her neighbors might well be the effort to which I devote the greatest part of my time, but in those days my primary concern, aside from my family, was trying to build up my business. I was on the road constantly, selling Slim-Mint and all our other Thompson Medical products. I used to travel four days a week, three weeks a month. I'd come back home on Thursday night, work on Friday, rest on Shabbat, and then go back to work on Sunday. In the spring of 1970, when I was approached by one of the leadership people in UJA about going on a mission to Israel, my first instinct was to say no. As it was, I was only home from business one full week a month, and now that would be the week I would travel to Israel. I was also sure my then wife, Estanne, would object to my leaving her alone with the four girls for yet another week. But to her credit she didn't object, and in May or June of 1970 I took off on a UJA mission for my first trip to Israel. My second day there, I visited the well-known Wingate Institute, Israel's great sports training center, in Netanya. I was looking for karate experts, whom I wanted to bring to the United States to help train Jewish kids in self-defense. I had long been obsessed with the notion of Jews being strong. It had often occurred to me that if the Jews in Europe had been better able to defend themselves against the Nazis, the Holocaust might not have happened. At Wingate, I learned for the first time about Krav Maga, a system of hand-to-hand combat that had been developed in Israel, and I made arrangements to have several teachers come to the United States to teach it to Jewish day school students.

But what really transformed my life was visiting the beach in Netanya. It does not sound dramatic. I walked to the beach, took a swim (which I loved to do), got dressed, and then had a steak sandwich in a pita at a kosher sidewalk café just off the beach. For me, that experience was very, very powerful. It reminded me of all that I had loved about my childhood in Long Beach. And being able to walk out of the water and have a kosher steak at a sidewalk café— that's something I'd never done in Long Beach. I felt as if I were in paradise. That night I called Estanne. "Get ready," I told her. "We're going to sell our apartment in New York and move to Israel."

I thought I was going to catch hell, but once again Estanne surprised me. "Okay," she said simply.

I immediately set out to find an apartment in Netanya, and located a beautiful building under construction, with a three-bedroom apartment and a terrace overlooking the blue Mediterranean for $40,000.

At the time, we owned a four-bedroom apartment with a Fifth Avenue exposure on Manhattan's East Side. A short time after my return to New York, we put the apartment on the market, but it wouldn't sell. This went on for well over a year. The apartment didn't end up selling until 1972, when a neighbor in the building bought it for $70,000, a price so low that it seems hard to believe from the perspective of 2009. Today it is probably worth $8 million.

We moved to Israel that same year, but our apartment in Netanya was not yet completed. Our first residence was an absorption center for new immigrants. The living accommodations were crowded; it was a two-bedroom apartment with a combined living-room/dining-room/kitchen. And we were a family of six. Still, starting our lives in a new country was very exciting. And sometimes very traumatic. One Saturday night I was saying *Havdala*, the prayer that is chanted at the Sabbath's end, when we heard a horrible crash outside the building. We rushed to the window and immediately saw that a bus had crushed a small car beneath it. At the time, there was no hospital in Netanya, and after a few minutes' wait we saw that no ambulance had arrived. I got into my station wagon, and a couple of new friends accompanied me as we took a little boy to the nearest hospital in Hadera, some twenty miles away. This is one of the nightmare memories of my life; by the time we reached Hadera Hospital, the child had died. The memory of that dead

"Growing up in Long Beach. From left to right (upper row): my sister, Judy, my mom, Stella, a young me; (bottom row): my dad, Sam, with my younger brother, Jerry, on his knee, and my older brother, Roy."

"An early picture with my loving younger brother, Jerry. Life is good."

"Army Days: Marseille, February 1945, (from left): me, Jerry Stein, and Danny Elster."

"With my sister, Judy, with whom I speak almost every day, and who loves to call me her older brother. But as this is a memoir, I need to set the record straight. I'm not."

"With Leah, Simmy, and Tammy, three of my four precious angels, during our seven remarkable years in Israel. Rebecca was probably out swimming."

"With Tammy and Simmy on a ski vacation. These vacations were so important to our family that I deferred my first trip to the Middle East with Congressman Wayne Owens because I didn't want to miss out on skiing with my super-fun daughters."

"Rebecca, Simmy, Leah, and Tammy, my four beautiful and loving daughters, on a March, 2009, visit to Palm Beach."

"I used to put up as many window signs for San-Cura—an anti-itch cream and my first product—as I could squeeze onto a store's window. Sometimes it seemed like the whole store was an anti-itch store. I would call the pharmacists 'Doc' and they would call me 'Itch.'"

"We marketed Slim-Fast as a Protein Diet powder and a Meal-in-a-Glass, and the sales took off. People wanted an uncomplicated diet that kept overweight people away from the temptation of solid foods for two meals a day, and thereby enabled them to lose pounds quickly."

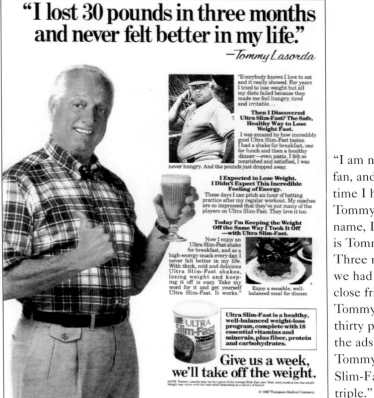

"I am not a baseball fan, and the first time I heard Tommy Lasorda's name, I asked, 'Who is Tommy Lasorda?' Three months later, we had become close friends, Tommy had lost thirty pounds, and the ads we did with Tommy caused Slim-Fast's sales to triple."

"My daughter Tammy working on a Slim-Fast ad. Not only is she a beautiful and loving daughter, but a great asset in helping me build our business. I was always impressed with Tammy's good eye and instinct for putting commercials together."

"Having fun—and I found business a lot of fun—with three of my favorite people: my beloved brother-in-law, Ed Steinberg, Tom Kemeny, and Dan Horwitz. Eddie has been a close and loving brother and friend for sixty-five years, and has been a help to me in everything I've done. He's the first one I always turn to."

Blackburn Named to S. Daniel Abraham Chair

Photo by Steve Gilbert

George Blackburn (right), an associate professor at HMS and Beth Israel Deaconess and director of the hospital's Center for the Study of Nutrition Medicine, was named the first incumbent of the S. Daniel Abraham Chair in Nutrition Medicine at HMS at a ceremony on December 7. As holder of the Abraham chair, Blackburn will continue his research on dietary fat and phytochemicals and their role in cancer growth.

S. Daniel Abraham (left), founder and chairman of Slim-Fast Foods Co. and Thompson Medical Co., endowed the chair. This is the second gift that Abraham has made to support nutrition studies at the Medical School.

"Dr. George Blackburn, one of my dearest and closest friends, and the man who always gave the best advice on how to maintain a high level of nutrition in Slim-Fast and also on how to keep me in the best physical condition. I was honored to be able to endow for George the S. Daniel Abraham Chair in Nutrition Medicine at Harvard Medical School, the position he has long occupied."

"With former President Bill Clinton, Ewa, Sarah, and Sam at the dedication of the Dan Abraham Healthy Living Center (October 23, 2007). The newspaper in Rochester, Minnesota, quoted me as saying it was 'one of the happiest days of my life.'"

"It gave me a lot of pleasure to see President Clinton working out, along with Beth Warren, head of the Living Center, and my good friend Jim Hodge, the Mayo Clinic's Chief of Development. I got a particular kick out of the president's comment during his speech that Dan Abraham 'makes health fanatics look like wussess compared to him.'"

"With Shimon Peres, Israel's former prime minister and now president. Shimon's vision of peace between Israel and her neighbors has long inspired me, and over the years our friendship has grown closer and closer."

"With three of the dearest loves of my life: Ewa, Sarah, and Sam."

child remains with me to this day, and one of the ways in which I responded to that catastrophe was by becoming active in helping to build Laniado Hospital in Netanya. Over the years, I have been very proud of my participation in this work. First, we dedicated a geriatric section, the Dan Abraham Geriatric Center. Israel had a lot of very difficult geriatric cases—people from all over Europe who had survived the Holocaust, who were not in good health when they made *aliyah*, and who deteriorated every year. At the center, I am proud to say, they were very well taken care of. We also were involved in the creation of a birthing and early pediatric care center. And the building of an operating theater, too.

But all this was in the future. Meanwhile, I needed to get active in business. When I left America, I had arranged to sell Thompson Medical to Dan Rodgers, my old friend and the former president of Revlon, for $250,000. I figured I could take the money, make 10 percent interest in the bank, and live like a king in Israel on $25,000 a year (what a difference in the value of a dollar then and now!). Only—at this point I don't remember why—Dan backed out of the deal. To which I can only say now, "Thank God." Thompson Medical later grew to have a value of over $200 million, and it was from Thompson Medical that we developed Slim-Fast. But that was all well in the future. At the time Dan backed out of the deal, I knew that I had to go back to earning my living from Thompson Medical— not the easiest thing to do while living in Israel. For one thing, I couldn't even get a telephone installed in our apartment. One widespread problem in Israel then was that waiting times for phones could be up to two years. In those days, they used to tell a joke in Israel about a new immigrant from the United States who orders a phone and is shocked when, after two weeks, it still hasn't arrived. In the United States at the time, you ordered a phone to be installed and two or three days later, you had it. Anyway, this new immigrant goes to the phone company, and asks why his phone hasn't arrived. The official looks at his records and says to the man, "But you only ordered it two weeks ago. Of course, it hasn't arrived."

The American is starting to despair. "How long will it take?"

The Israeli shrugs. "Many, many months."

"You mean I have no hope of getting a phone sooner," the American says.

The Israeli looks at him piously. "It is forbidden for a Jew to say he has no hope. No chance maybe, but never say no hope."

So I had no chance—or hope—of getting a phone installed in our home quickly, but I learned that I could rent office space that already had a phone. So I did— the only time in my life I had to rent an office just to have access to a phone. But I had no choice: I spent hours a day on that phone doing business on behalf of Thompson Medical, talking to our people in New York and customers throughout the United States.

In 1972, we were doing $2 million a year in total revenue, and making $100,000 in pretax earnings. The good news was, though, that the company grew a lot from 1972 to 1978, the years I lived in Israel (and I only moved back because the time commitments to Thompson were becoming too overwhelming). When I returned to the United States in 1978, we were doing $40 million in revenue. A short time later, we took Thompson Medical public, selling 25 percent of the company for $10 million. That was the first time in my life I had real money.*

Meanwhile, I quickly became involved in starting a small synagogue in Netanya. We rented a space and soon prepared to start our congregation on the Shabbat after Yom Kippur, 1973. That Yom Kippur was, of course, the day that Egypt and Syria attacked Israel, launching the Yom Kippur War. I remember being in services that Yom Kippur at a friend's synagogue as men were called out, one after another, and summoned to their army units. By the end of the day, almost all the Israeli men were gone.

During the Yom Kippur War, I volunteered to do whatever I could. My most meaningful job was help-ing to refuel the American planes that were flying into

---

*Ten years later, we took the company private again, for $150 mil-lion. So it was a good investment for anyone who bought shares in Thompson Medical. Going private was also good for me, since only a few days after we bought back the company, Oprah made her announcement about her sixty-pound weight loss on Optifast, an announcement that caused a tremendous increase in Slim-Fast's sales (see page 119). Our decision to go private at that time was a happy coincidence; we had no idea about Oprah's upcoming an-nouncement and the effect it would have on our business, but it was indeed a lucky break.

Israel with desperately needed weapons and other supplies for the Israeli army. The first weeks of the war had gravely depleted Israel's armaments, and when President Richard Nixon authorized the airlift to Israel, Prime Minister Golda Meir regarded it as a life-saver. It was remarkable to watch the procession of American planes setting down every fifteen minutes, and to then see the crews, operating with remarkable precision, wheeling off giant containers of ammunition and weapons (and loading back on Soviet-made equipment that Israel had captured on the field; the U.S. military wanted to see the new tanks and radar stations the Soviets had sent Egypt to use against Israel). My job was a basic one—to hook up the hose to refuel the planes. It was very moving for me, seeing the two countries I most loved in the world working together in tandem. I was so proud of those American planes and soldiers.

That first Saturday after Yom Kippur we had to decide if we wanted to start a new synagogue in the middle of a war. And we decided that we did. On Shabbat, we hosted many soldiers on weekend leave, and the synagogue continued very successfully after that.

My youngest daughter at the time, Simmy, was only two when we moved to Israel (Rebecca was eight, Laurie seven, and Tammy five). I remember our concern when we enrolled Simmy in preschool: She was unnaturally quiet. The reason soon became apparent. Until she started preschool, Simmy had lived in a house where only English was spoken; now, she suddenly found herself in an exclusively Hebrew-speaking environment. What a miracle it was three months later when she started speaking in school and her Hebrew was perfect. I just wish my Hebrew were as good.

I loved my life in Netanya, and in Israel in general. Getting involved in helping to build Laniado Hospital and then becoming involved in volunteer work during the Yom Kippur War and helping build up our new synagogue got me increasingly involved in Israeli communal life. The Bible teaches, "It is not good for man to be alone"; indeed, that's the first thing the Bible says is not good. And wherever I have lived, I've always tried to get involved in building up the community.

After the Yom Kippur War, I slowly started to become involved in Israeli political life as well. General Ariel Sharon, who had won such a following in Israel after he and his troops crossed the Suez Canal in one of the Yom Kippur War's crucial battles, formed a new political party, ShlomTzion (Peace for Zion). Everything I learned about Sharon impressed me, and I sought him out and offered to work for his party. Whatever expertise I had developed over the years in writing ads I applied now to helping Sharon's campaign. I even paid to run a couple of ads on his party's behalf. We became friends then, and our friendship lasted for over thirty years, until the terrible stroke that has left him comatose since 2006. There were many lighthearted moments in our years of friendship, but the most poignant occurred in the aftermath of his beloved wife Lili's death in 2002. Sharon had already become prime minister, and was visiting the United States. He invited me to his hotel room, and we spoke for over an hour. At the end of our conversation, I asked him, "How can I be of help to you?" He replied, "Just be my friend. Just be my friend."

What beautiful words, and they really touched me.

As is apparent, I loved being in Israel. The very thing that originally sold me on Netanya—that swim at the beach—continued to attract me. Every day I would walk down to the beach—even during the winter when there were heavy storms—climbing down the hundred steps from the cliff near our house. I would jump into the water. It wasn't always the smartest thing to do. One winter day I took an extended swim. The water was so cold it seemed to me I could feel my brain freezing. When I got back upstairs, my heart started pumping very loudly. I quickly visited my physician, who told me I had developed a heart arrhythmia: My heart had been shocked out of rhythm. I didn't want to start any medications (particularly after my doctor told me I would have to take them for the rest of my life), so I decided to try to get my rhythm restored through exercise. I started exercising heavily, doing a variety of things, including jumping jacks, and bending down and touching my toes. Eventually, my heart rhythm returned to normal without the need for medications.

One aspect of life in Israel was traumatic. It seemed as if terrorist attacks were a permanent part of the country's landscape. During our years in Netanya we lived next door to the Park Hotel. Twenty-five years later one of the worst attacks of the Second Intifada occurred at the hotel. A suicide bombing was carried out during a Passover seder in which thirty people were blown up. But even during the mid-1970s there were brutal and very lethal attacks. In one awful incident, terrorists broke into an Israeli apartment in Naharia and murdered a baby by throwing the child off the apartment's terrace. At the time, I put up a steel door at our apartment's entrance, with special security bolts. It gave my family a tremendously increased sense of security, and to this day I have security doors wherever I live.

I really loved raising my children in a friendly, warm, beach community, and forming wonderful friendships. Unfortunately, though, the pressures of running a business from six thousand miles away were too onerous. As much as I used the phone to stay in touch, I needed to make face-to-face contacts as well. At first, I started going back to the States each month for six days at a time, then it was two trips of six days each. Between the eleven-hour plane ride four times a month and the seven-hour time difference—and the time away from my family—it was very difficult.

By 1978, it was apparent that we would have to return to the United States. I kept the apartment in Netanya, and three of my daughters ended up living in Israel for many years. One of my daughters still lives in Netanya. As much as I love the United States, part of my heart has always remained nostalgic for that time in Netanya, for the time in Israel. There's a famous line of the medieval Hebrew poet, Judah Halevi, "I am in the West, but (part of) my heart is in the East"—particularly on a beach in Netanya, and at a sidewalk café.

AFTERWORD

As is clear, my love of and devotion to the country remained with me even after I moved back to the United States. Some ten years later, starting with a meeting with Congressman Wayne Owens (D-Utah), I had an opportunity to try to do something tangible for Israel, by helping to engage in a process that could bring about peace between Israel and her neighbors.

My efforts, together with Wayne, started with a trip to Egypt in 1988, and eventually resulted in the creation of the Center for Middle East Peace and Economic Cooperation in Washington, D.C. Our friendship and partnership also led to dozens of trips to the Middle East, and to over a thousand meetings. Among those with whom we often met were Egyptian president Hosni Mubarak, Syrian president Hafez Assad, Jordan's King Hussein, Crown Prince—later King—Abdullah of Saudi Arabia, and many meetings with Yasser Arafat. At the same time, I established ongoing and often close relationships with the various Israeli prime ministers, including Shimon Peres, Yitchak Shamir, Yitchak Rabin, Benjamin Netanyahu, Ariel Sharon, Ehud Olmert, and Ehud Barak. And of course I am also very proud of our close-working relationship with high-ranking U.S. government officials really too numerous to mention.

I wrote about the nature of these meetings in my earlier book, *Peace Is Possible* (New York: Newmarket, 2006), and intend to elaborate on my thoughts on how a peace settlement can be achieved now in an upcoming book, *The Prize Is Worth the Price*.

X

"The Happiest Day of My Life": What I Have Learned about the Pleasure of Giving

My grandson asked me recently, "What was the happiest day of your life?" And I said, "Today." Because every day should be a happy day. You should always be doing things that are important to you, things that make you happy.

But even among happy days, some are more memorable than others. Something that happened just a few years ago brought me—and continues to bring me—a particular sense of satisfaction.

It all started in the early 1990s, when I developed a cough. That sounds like a small matter, but it wasn't. At first, the cough was just irritating, as all coughs are, but this one soon became hacking and painful; it also brought up a lot of disgusting-looking phlegm. Over the coming two years, a dozen physicians examined me and put me on a variety of antibiotics, but none helped. What became apparent was that none of the doctors could accurately identify the infection causing the cough. At one point during this period I was in a milk-processing plant in Holland, near Amsterdam. We were working on improving the taste of Slim-Fast, but I just sat at the table coughing and coughing. It was an awful experience. I drank a lot of water, and eventually the coughing eased. But soon it was back full force.

My inability to recover from the cough—even after two years—was both very unpleasant and increasingly worrisome. Then, in September 1993, I was sitting with hundreds of others on the White House lawn watching the signing of the Oslo Peace Accords by Israeli Prime Minister Yitzhak Rabin and Palestinian Chairman Yasser Arafat, in the presence of President Bill Clinton. There was a U.S. ambassador to one of the Caribbean islands sitting next to me. She heard my persistent coughing and when I told her how long it had been going on, she urged me to call the Mayo Clinic in Rochester, Minnesota. At the time, I had heard of Mayo, though I didn't know much about it. But this ambassador spoke of her treatment there with such enthusiasm that right after the signing I called up and made an appointment for the following day.

It was quickly determined that, in order to make a proper diagnosis, my lungs needed to be biopsied. It took a full two weeks to grow the harmful bacteria in my lungs. Dr. Udaya Prakash, the pulmonologist who treated me, was then finally able to offer what had eluded all my previous physicians—an accurate diagnosis. He informed me that I was suffering from a rare bacteria in the pseudomonas family (something that could have been fatal). Fortunately there was one antibiotic effective against it. I started taking it immediately and, within two or three days, this cough—which had been weakening me so much for over two years—was gone. The sense of relief was amazing.

A short time later, when another health issue arose, I went back to Mayo. This time, I also arranged to meet with Laird Yock, a member of the Development Office, who took me on a walk around the grounds. Mayo had been remarkable to me, and I wanted to give something back. I knew that I wasn't in a position at that point in my life to donate an entire building, which is what the Mayo Clinic's biggest givers did. I also knew that I wanted to give a different sort of gift, something to benefit the staff, the health givers, not just the patients. The Mayo Clinic has more than 25,000 employees ministering to patients' needs. But when I saw the condition of these employees themselves, from a health standpoint, it wasn't great. Many of them were very heavy and out of shape. I knew from my own experience at Mayo that the patients there already have access to the best medical facility, but many of the employees weren't taking care of themselves. So, on that very first walk, I shared with Yock—and subsequently, Jim Hodge with whom I became very close—my impressions of the employees' situation, and said that I wanted to do something for them. "Build a health facility," he told me. "That'll help them."

This made sense. After all, my work on Slim-Fast had come about because I was very committed to helping people lose excess weight and become healthy and fit. So I said to him, "Why don't we put up a healthy living center?" That was the term that occurred to me on the spot, and it's been the term we've used ever since. I still remember exactly what I was thinking: *It is the people who work at Mayo who make all the difference. Let's do something to make them feel invigorated and good about themselves, and then they will carry that good feeling into their work and to their families.*

Over the coming years, we opened two exercise facilities, one on the downtown campus (1995), and the second at St. Mary's Hospital (1998). I was pleased to see how widely used both sites were, but I also knew that they were still only reaching a relatively small, and perhaps already motivated, proportion of the employees.

My goals eventually grew more ambitious—to open a facility for many thousands of people and to have that facility exemplify the concept of healthy living centers all over the United States. It's in everybody's interests to help keep employees healthy. The people who work at Mayo devote their working lives to helping sick people get well. Don't they deserve to have a facility to keep them healthier and help stop them from becoming sick? In addition, the advantages from such a program would benefit their employers and the broader society as well. Healthy employees feel physically better, have higher self-esteem, work more productively, and have longer work lives. It's a win-win situation, and that's why I hoped a larger, more wide-ranging facility would also serve as a model for other large companies on how to help their employees become and stay well. It would also spur doctors to encourage their patients to adopt lifestyle changes to promote wellness. Getting people well when they're sick should be a primary, but not *the* primary, goal of the medical profession. The first objective of medicine should be to keep people healthy and to keep them from becoming ill. Right now the United States is spending over $1 trillion to get our economy back to health. But we spend over $2 trillion a year on our health care system—twice per capita as any other developed nation. So one of my goals is not only to help strengthen the health givers, but also to start bringing Mayo patients and visitors into the facility and to teach them how to live a healthy life.

In any case, it was from this sort of thinking, developed in conjunction with the people at Mayo—particularly Jim Hodge—that the idea grew for what eventually became the Dan Abraham Healthy Living Center.

DAHLC, as it is known, opened on September 4, 2007, and was officially dedicated seven weeks later, on October 23. That is the day one local newspaper said I had called "the happiest day of my life." I flew up to Mayo with my wife, Ewa, and our two beautiful children, Sarah and Sam. Eddie and Judy Steinberg, my sister and brother-in-law, were also there, the two people who have been with me literally since the day we bought San-Cura sixty years earlier. One of their daughters, Marilyn Lauer, came in as well. My brother Jerry was among the attendees, along with his son Sam. My daughter Tammy was there with her husband, Carey, as well as Yaakov Pinck, my oldest and very close grandchild, and Dr. George Blackburn, one of my oldest and closest friends. Yoni Komorov, my loyal and extremely competent personal aide came, along with Rabbi Josh Lookstein, a great friend, who was heading my foundation. And most fittingly, Charles Davis, along with his son Jordan, was there. Charles is my physical trainer—he puts me through quite a rigorous daily workout—and he had trained and worked at Mayo for fifteen years before he came to work with me. He is an extremely talented and dedicated physical therapist.

A gathering of so many of the people whom I care about deeply was one important element in what made this day so special. Included in that list of people for whom I have deep affection and gratitude are the dozens of doctors at Mayo who have cared for my health over the last fifteen years, physicians who have treated my heart, dealt with issues of dermatology and high blood pressure, spinal problems, and a seriously injured knee.

Another exciting highlight of that day was being publicly lauded by a man whom I deeply love and admire. "I thank you for giving me the opportunity to be here today," former President Clinton began his speech that morning. "Danny Abraham has given me a lot of opportunities. He has been my generous friend, he has been a friend to my wife and to our family, but having the opportunity to come to the Mayo Clinic for this occasion today is particularly important for me at this time in my life and [for] the work that I do now. I think that first we ought to acknowledge the success of the Mayo Clinic in treating Mr. Abraham." I got a real kick out of his next line, particularly since it was delivered in the presence of so many hundreds of people: "He is the youngest person his age on the planet. He makes health fanatics anywhere look like wusses compared to him." He then went on to praise me in a way that really moved me, as he understood the full essence of what I hoped this health center would accomplish: "He wants the opportunities, the habits, the state of mind that have given him the rich long life he's had to be available to every human being in this country and across the globe."*

It wasn't just President Clinton who understood the significance of what I hoped this new facility would accomplish. Dr. Denis Cortese, the president and CEO of the Mayo Clinic, said that day, "The Dan Abraham Healthy Living Center is an outward expression of our vision to improve the health of our employees, our nation, and the world." And the center's medical director, Dr. Kerry Olsen, spoke of DAHLC not just as a workout facility, "but as the newest medical facility on Mayo's campus."

The center itself contains four floors, filled with state-of-the-art fitness equipment, and staffed with fitness professionals who provide one-on-one wellness assessments, coaching, and personal training.

The center is headed by Beth Warren, a woman for whom I have great admiration and who is perfect at what she does. The DAHLC staff work out an action plan with each new member. They provide group exercise classes, Pilates, and yoga, even healthy cooking

---

* I also received an unusual compliment from Dr. Amir Lerman, my cardiologist—and good friend—at Mayo: "I realize that. . . I may be expected to know the most about your heart. And truly, Dan, you have one of the best and kindest hearts that I have come across, and it has been a real pleasure and an honor to be taking care of it."

classes. One thing that makes DAHLC different from traditional gyms is its emphasis on enlisting sedentary and overweight individuals, the type of people who shy away from gyms. These are exactly the sort of people we reach out to, and it's a common sight to see a person walking for the first time on an indoor track alongside an experienced marathon runner who is training to lower her running time by five minutes. In addition to the obvious inducements of becoming healthier, we also built in financial incentives to encourage people to come back often: The more times you exercise in a month, the less you pay (the center is, in any case, priced very reasonably, between $15 and $25 a month per employee).

In its first six months of operation, more than 15,000 members enrolled in the new center, and today as many as 3,600 people pass through its doors daily; recently, an eight-week weight-management class was announced on the center's Web site, and it became fully subscribed within ten minutes. All this gives me such a great sense of satisfaction. As I've long known, and as my work with DAHLC has reminded me again: "When you give, you always get back more than you gave." Some people think that adage is one of those hackneyed clichés that doesn't hold up to scrutiny. Believe me, it does. How could I not think so when I look back at the hundreds and hundreds of letters of gratitude I have received since the center's opening? One woman, a longtime nurse at Mayo, wrote to tell me of fellow employees "waiting by the door at 5 a.m. to start their healthy day." She also wrote that "It is wonderful for our patients to see healthy people [working at

Mayo]. As you know, when people feel good about themselves, it shows throughout their work. We love those workout endorphins." Another employee wrote to tell me how she and her husband, Jim, love the "Dan Abraham Healthy Living Center, and use this beautiful facility three, four, and five times weekly. We are so thankful for all these opportunities to keep active and healthy."

The letters continue to arrive. Here's one that was sent to me just a few weeks ago, in early 2009 (I've only deleted information that could point to the writer's identity).

Dear Dan,

I'm a lawyer from ____, Florida. I am sitting in your healthy living center in Rochester. My husband was diagnosed with multiple myeloma and received a stem cell transplant. I have been here for a month. If it were not for your great center, there is no way I could have dealt with the stress of my husband's medical issue. I have spent twenty-five years representing clients who have cancer against polluters and am so aware of how stress takes a toll on life.

What a great gift you have given Mayo. Thank you from my heart. Thank you again for the difference you have made in so many lives.

Over the years, I've gotten a great kick out of hearing that employees at Mayo often refer to the health center as "The Dan." What a nice association to have with my name, and one given to me by people who devote their lives to saving lives. "The Dan." What a great tribute!

XI

What Judaism Has Taught Me

As I've already noted, I grew up in a traditional Jewish home. We kept Shabbat and *kashrut* (kosher laws), went to synagogue on the Sabbath, and every night before going to sleep I said the *Sh'ma** and added on a personal prayer to God to protect my father and mother, my siblings, me, America, and the Jewish people. My view of God was a common one, that He intervenes in each person's life, and that if you pray to Him there is a good chance He will answer your prayers.

My World War II battle experiences strongly challenged that belief. I admit that during the war, when I was being shelled, I would pray over and over, "God

---

* *Sh'ma Yisrael.* The *Sh'ma*, the most famous prayer and statement of faith in Judaism, is translated as follows: "Hear O Israel, the Lord is Our God, the Lord is One," followed by a paragraph that starts with "Thou shall love the Lord your God with all your heart, with all you soul and with all your might."

save me, please, God save me, God save me, please, please." There's a lot of truth to the old expression, "There are no atheists in foxholes." But, eventually, too many battles left their mark, and I came out of the war believing that God does not pick and choose who gets killed, and He does not protect the innocent or punish the guilty, at least not in this world (and that's where we live). I can understand believing that there is a supernatural power that created this earth, planted it here, and put it into orbit, along with the sun and all the planets. What I find far harder to believe is that there is a God who watches over each person, and not only over each individual human being but over each animal, and seventy million years ago over each dinosaur. It's very hard for me to believe that some force exists that has that sort of consciousness and involvement. And honestly, if God does intervene in each life, I have not seen enough evidence of it to convince me. When you're getting bombed on a battlefield and people near you are losing limbs and others are losing their lives, it becomes very hard to believe that there is a God directing where each bomb explodes. Sometimes, when I puzzle over these things, I try to remind myself that the reason Jewish men wear a yarmulke is that the mind can only go so far.

Ever since those army years, and especially the Holocaust and the human tragedies of the war, I've struggled with issues of faith and doubt, and with some other aspects of Judaism as well. As I mentioned, while I was in the army I didn't follow Jewish laws much. When I had the chance, like over Yom Kippur in Florence, I went to synagogue services, and it felt very good. But I ate all the food the army served (although I ate ham, I didn't eat bacon because I feared I would like it too much and not be able to give it up later), and after I was discharged from the army I continued eating nonkosher food. Even in my least observant days, some aspects of *kashrut* (kosher laws) remained with me, the most prominent being that I wouldn't mix meat with milk, a trademark feature of all kosher homes. Strangely enough, because I held on to that one observance, I eventually found my way back to keeping kosher. The first office I rented in Manhattan for Thompson Medical was right over a restaurant called Ryan's Rest, a diner run by two delightful Irish guys—brothers. Both brothers were very kind to me, and used to take care of my mail and packages. There were many days when I ate breakfast, lunch, and dinner at the restaurant. It was twenty-five cents for a hamburger, and five cents for each vegetable. I still recall the evening I was eating oxtail ragout, which was delicious, and drinking tea with it. I would have preferred coffee, but I only like coffee with milk, and I wouldn't mix meat with milk. I said to myself, *Danny, what are you doing? Here you are, eating* treif *(nonkosher) meat, and you're worried about mixing it with milk. What sense does that make?*

To this day, I remember the next thought I had: *Before I give up on Judaism and Jewish laws, I owe it to my parents and ancestors, who brought these traditions to me through thousands of years, to find out whether these traditions still make sense for a young Jew in twentieth-century America.* I had to learn a lot more about the meaning of Jewish traditions. I went to the Jewish Theological

Seminary, largely because that was the only Jewish educational facility with which I was familiar, and took an evening course in basic Hebrew. There, I met a group of young people I became friendly with. They said, "Why don't you come with us to the Young Israel on 16th Street. There's a rabbi there who gives courses in Jewish philosophy." That sounded wonderful to me, because the questions that were bothering me were more likely to be addressed in a philosophy course than in a class on basic Hebrew. The rabbi at Young Israel, an Orthodox organization, was Isaac Swift. He was a great teacher. I asked all the questions I had about religion: Does Shabbat make sense? Do the holidays make sense? Do the Jewish laws and ways of giving charity make sense? Does keeping kosher make sense? Because of my religious doubts, what I was really trying to figure out was what aspects of Judaism would make sense and still be valid even if there were no God. Because the God issue—then and now, too—was problematic for me.... How could God permit six million people to go to their deaths in the Holocaust? Certainly they were not being punished for something they did. And it was not just the Holocaust. In World War II alone, almost sixty million people were killed—many, if not most of them, civilians—men, women, and children. There were plenty of other injustices in the world that couldn't be explained, including infants born crippled or blind or severely retarded. And if God doesn't play an active role in our lives, why believe? I mean, you can believe in Him if you want, but either way the same thing is going to happen whether you pray or not.

I don't remember Rabbi Swift offering any answers on the God issue that put my doubts to rest. But what he had to say about Jewish laws—like observing Shabbat and the holidays, giving charity, and keeping kosher—made a great deal of sense. I also liked that I could argue with him; he didn't cut off questioning. During one class he expressed the belief, common in the Orthodox world, that the Temple in Jerusalem be rebuilt, and sacrifices be reinstituted. I said to him, "Are you crazy? In the twentieth century, that will never happen." But Rabbi Swift didn't backtrack. He said, "It's better to kill an animal, because that helps get the bloodlust out of human beings. Look what's going on all over the world, and look at the war that just ended. People were killing people everywhere." I don't say that his reasoning convinced me—even if sacrifices had done some good in the past, I certainly didn't want to see them reinstituted now—but I loved being in an atmosphere in which Judaism was discussed seriously, and in which rationales for why Jewish law should still be observed were offered.

Those classes with Rabbi Swift influenced me a lot, though, for me, returning to a religious lifestyle was a multiyear effort, and one that has had its ups and downs. But ever since that time I have always kept kosher, not the easiest thing when you travel to so many countries like I do. But my hosts know that I don't eat nonkosher meat or shellfish and go out of their way to prepare fish and vegetable dishes for me.

I also started to observe the Sabbath laws, one of the most well-known of which is the prohibition on driving. I remember when Vice President Al Gore vis-

ited Palm Beach and I took him to services at Temple
Emmanuel. Afterwards, he prepared to come back to
my house for lunch, and he invited me to join him in
his car. I told him I didn't drive on the Sabbath and
Jewish holidays, so he walked home with me. I find
that if I'm upfront and unembarrassed about my Jewish
observances, it makes other people feel fully comfortable with them.

On the other hand, there are certain Sabbath rituals
that I've grown more liberal about observing over the
years. For example, the Torah explicitly forbids lighting a fire on the Sabbath: "You shall kindle no fire . . .
on the Sabbath day" (Exodus 35:3). I strictly observe
this law, and wouldn't light a stove, for example, on the
Sabbath. However, for over a century, since electricity
was created, Orthodox Judaism has equated electricity
with fire, and forbids its usage on the Sabbath. That's
why many Orthodox Jews have timers in their homes,
popularly known as "Shabbes clocks," which turn off
lights late Friday night, and turn them on again on Saturday afternoon. The same is done on the other biblical
holidays. In my stricter days of observance, I was very
careful not to use electricity. I tell the story later of the
Sukkot holiday when I confronted a neo-Nazi rally in
New York (see pages 191-194), and how, after attending
synagogue services, I had walked up eighteen flights to
get to my apartment in Manhattan that evening. It was
only when I arrived upstairs and went out on my patio
that I heard this pro-Nazi ranting on a loudspeaker. So
I walked down eighteen floors again, and then, after a
confrontation, back up the eighteen flights.

I would like to believe that had skyscrapers existed in the past, the rabbis might have ruled differently about elevators. And the truth is that, in cities like New York, filled with observant Jews and very tall buildings, many people arrange for their non-Jewish doormen to push the button for their floor (it's forbidden to let fellow Jews violate the Sabbath or holiday laws for you, since they are as bound by the laws as you are). Since non-Jews are not obligated to observe the Sabbath, there is no problem with their pushing the button. But Jewish law gets very complicated, and a Jew is not supposed to explicitly ask a non-Jew to push the button for him. Most doormen learn that when observant Jewish residents come in, they should just go over and press the button for them. As you can see, these laws can sometimes get pretty convoluted. In my own life, I decided at some point that there is a difference between electricity and fire, and that in this day and age I would have to push the button myself.

Strangely—or maybe not so strangely—despite my doubts about God, I have always considered the Torah a great guide for life. It is the one book I have read and studied again and again, and because I attend services almost every Shabbat, I end up rereading a good part of the Torah every year. While it's being chanted during the service, I like to read the various commentaries, among them the ArtScroll edition and the Hertz Chumash (*Chumash*, which comes from the Hebrew word for "five," is the Hebrew term for the Five Books of Moses).

Many of the Torah's lessons have affected me both in terms of how I behave and also in terms of how I view the world. For example, the Bible teaches that if you have a farm, when you harvest the crops, you should leave part of the harvest in the field for the poor, and let the poor glean from what has been left behind. Today, when I pass an obviously very poor or homeless person on the street, I always give them some dollars. The Torah also calls on people to donate 10 percent of what they produce to support the poor.

As these laws demonstrate, Judaism is very concerned about doing good deeds. The most famous law in the Torah is "Love your neighbor as yourself" (Leviticus 19:18). When the first century spiritual leader Rabbi Hillel was asked by a non-Jew who wished to convert to Judaism to summarize Judaism while he was standing on one foot, Hillel answered, "What's hateful to you, don't do to your neighbor. The rest is commentary. Now, go and study" (Babylonian Talmud, *Shabbat* 31a).

Another passage from the Torah that has long moved me is the one in which Moses, while on the holy mountain, tells God, "I want to see Your face." It would seem that what Moses wanted was to truly know God. But God says to Moses, "You can't see Me face-to-face and live; you can only see Me from the back." God responds to Moses's request by putting him in the cleft of the rock. He puts His hand over Moses, passes by, and then takes His hand away and tells Moses that he can now see Him from the rear. As I understand it, God, in not allowing Moses to see God's face, was telling him that you can't see what God is going to do, but only what God has already done. To know God, therefore, means to know Him through what He has done; that is, through His actions.

Torah texts lend themselves to so many interpretations. One of the great rabbinic teachers of modern Jewish life, Rabbi Emmanuel Rackman, draws a fascinating lesson from God's permitting Moses only to see Him from the rear: "Recognition from the rear does not yield more than a relative amount of certainty and that is the maximum we humans can expect vis-à-vis God. God may have had His own reasons for denying us certainty with regard to His existence and nature. One reason apparent to us is that man's certainty with regard to anything is poison to his soul."

A further lesson from the Bible: The Torah teaches that God created everything. For instance, "And God said, 'Let there be light,' and there was light" (Genesis 1:3). God created the world, He created animal and vegetable life, and He created man. It seems to me that the first way to show love to God (another Torah verse commands, "And you shall love the Lord your God" [Deuteronomy 6:5]) is to show gratitude for these gifts. One way to show gratitude is through prayer, thanking God for the beautiful life and the beautiful world He has given us. Just as important as prayer, I believe, is enjoying life. After all, God is the giver of many wonderful gifts, most important life itself, and when you give a gift, you want the recipient to enjoy it, to derive pleasure from it. God wants us to enjoy the world.

Yet another way to show gratitude to God is to take very good care of His gifts. That is the basis for my strong belief in taking care of, and not exploiting,

God's earth. When God looks down on this world, I want Him to be able to say to humankind, "Not only did you enjoy my world, but you took care of it. Look how beautiful it is!" So we should do something every day to make the world a better, happier place.

Showing respect for God's creation also means treating all life with respect. This, I believe, applies to every creature. For example, God gave life to an ant, so don't take its life away, because to take any life unnecessarily is to destroy a creature to whom God gave life. The Torah does permit the eating of meat, and I've never been a vegetarian. But even in this case, the Torah places restrictions. The animal has to be treated with respect, dignity, and compassion. For example, Jewish law rules that the knife used to slaughter an animal must be totally sharp and smooth—no notches—so that the animal dies instantaneously.

I repeatedly study the Torah to learn from its teachings the sort of life I want to lead. Take the Tenth Commandment, one which is spoken of far less often than the Fifth ("Honor your father and mother") and the Sixth ("You shall not murder"). The Tenth Commandment forbids coveting your neighbor's property or your neighbor's possessions. This is just the sort of law whose observance leads to a happier life and to a well-balanced society. If all of us went around coveting our neighbor's possessions, we would not be good neighbors to each other. If your neighbor has more than you, it's all right for you to want more, but not for the sake of having more than he does and certainly what is his. You can be happy with what you have, be happy with your wife and your house, without having to have more than someone else.

While I am more familiar with Torah laws (of which there are 613), I have also been influenced by the laws of the Talmud, and medieval rabbinic scholars like Maimonides. There is a teaching in the Talmud that was made famous by Maimonides. In setting down the laws of charity, he listed the eight best ways to practice charity. If you ask people to guess which way is the highest form of charity, most will say anonymous giving. But that's not the Jewish teaching (in any case, the most important anonymity in Jewish sources is not that of the giver but of the recipient). But Maimonides argues that the highest form of charitable giving is to lend people money to help them establish themselves in business.

That law certainly influenced my father. As I mentioned earlier, when I was a teenager, I started a newspaper, which I printed on a mimeograph machine. The machine cost $25, which was an impossibly high sum for me to put together in the late 1930s when I started the paper. My father, though not rich, could have simply bought me a mimeograph machine. But he didn't. In his wisdom, he loaned me the $25, and I paid him back twenty-five cents a week for a hundred weeks. He certainly knew his son, and I learned a lot from that experience, The most important lessons I drew from that loan: Don't depend in life on gifts and handouts. And run your business responsibly, so that you can pay off any debts you've incurred.

One particular Jewish teaching has particular significance today—the belief that life is the highest value.

The rabbis of the Talmud hold that when life is threatened, other laws are suspended. That's why the most ritually observant Jews will get into a car on Saturday if severe illness makes it necessary for them to get to a hospital, or to help someone else do so.

Among the talmudic teachings that have most influenced and shaped me are a series of questions and answers in the book *Pirkei Avot, the Ethics of the Fathers*. This is a collection of the greatest thoughts of the rabbis of the Talmud. It is in this book, for example, that you find Hillel's teaching, "If I am not for myself, who will be for me? And if I am only for myself, what am I?" And then his great conclusion, "If not now, when?" In the fourth chapter of *Ethics of the Fathers*, one rabbi, Ben Zoma, poses a succession of probing questions. They all have profound answers. One is, "Who is rich?" The answer offered: "One who is happy with what he has." I don't know whether or not it's because of that teaching or because of my general nature, but I find that I'm happy most of the time.... The large majority of things that happen to us in this world are in our hands, and come about as a result of what we have done. Those of us who are happy, therefore, are those who are happy with the choices we have made. I know that in my own life I've learned to be happy with what I have. And this was true well before I had a lot of money. My son-in-law Carey Wolchok was speaking with Monroe Milstein, the founder of the Burlington Coat Factory and a man who grew up with me in Long Beach. Carey told me that Monroe recalls seeing me frequently riding my bike on the Long Beach Boardwalk and that, without fail, I always had a smile on my face.

Another question, asked and answered by the rabbi, is "Who is wise?" The answer: "One who learns from everyone." Again, excellent advice. But the question and answer that has most influenced me is "Who is strong?" To which Ben Zoma responds: "He who controls himself." Strength involves controlling your own behavior. This has been a recurring theme in my life. For example, I try never to get angry, but rather to always show a more positive side of myself. I try to do so even when I'm provoked.

Ben Zoma was right. Strength depends on controlling your passions. When I was in business, there were times employees acted carelessly and did something that could have, and should have, been avoided. But I worked on controlling myself. When a show of some unhappiness on my part was necessary, I tried at most to present myself as angry even when I wasn't truly angry. Years later, a friend told me that this was the position taken by Maimonides, the greatest medieval Jewish philosopher and the rabbi who wrote a fourteen-volume work, called the Mishneh Torah, codifying all of Jewish law. In one section of his code, *Hilchot De'ot*, dealing with character development, Maimonides writes that even when anger is justified, such as when your children have acted wrongly and you wish to return them to the right path, you should present yourself as angry but "inwardly you should be calm" (2:3). In other words, you should be like an actor who is playing the role of an angry person: Your anger should have one goal—to prevent the problem from recurring. But when anger becomes unrestrained, you end up yelling, humiliating, and provoking anger in the other person, and this leads to a worse situation, not a better one.

One of my daughters—I'm certainly not going to mention which one—used to provoke me when she was very young. A few times—not often—I spanked her lightly, convinced that she could control what she was doing if only she wanted to. At the time, I was seeing Dr. Saul Heller, the psychiatrist I mentioned earlier and a man who always offered me wise counsel. Dr. Heller said to me, "Well, when you spank her, does she stop provoking you?" I said, "No," and he said, "So why do you do it?" To express anger when it does no good is obviously wrong, and I immediately stopped.

Yet another area in which I learned to control my inclinations is a little—just a little—embarrassing to write about. But it was important to me, and might be helpful to others as well. There came a time in my life when I was drinking more liquor than I should have. As my friend, Dr. George Blackburn, tactfully put it, "It's not bringing out the best in you. There is nothing redeeming for who you want to be that you're gaining by drinking. It is destructive."

I spoke about it with the psychiatrist I was seeing at the time, Dr. Ed Stevens. He already knew that I drank too much; we had discussed it before. There was one session I had with him when Dr. Stevens tried to convince me that I was an alcoholic. I didn't like the idea of being an alcoholic, and denied it. I could control my drinking, I insisted. I simply drank because I enjoyed it. He said, "Well, then, if you can control your drinking, why don't you try going thirty days without a drink, and if you don't like what you feel like, go back to drinking.

Just quit for thirty days." At the end of the session, he said to me, "Danny, are you going to do this?" And I said, "Well, I'll tell you what. I'll try tonight."

I had a boat at the time, it was on the 79th Street pier on the Hudson River and Dr. Stevens's office was on 79th Street around Sixth Avenue. I walked from his office to the boat; I had a party on the boat that night for Lubavitch (Chabad-Lubavitch, a worldwide Hasidic organization), and Bibi Netanyahu was the speaker. I didn't know Bibi at the time. He was the Israeli Ambassador to the U.N., and today he is the Prime Minister of Israel and a good friend. Whenever I went to a party or a function like that, a cocktail party, I had to have a drink in my hand. So I came to the dock and the steward who used to serve drinks at my parties met me on the dock with a glass of vodka on the rocks. I said to him, "I'm not drinking tonight." He was so shocked that he dropped the glass on the dock, and it shattered. I'll never forget that—the drink just fell out of his hand. It made me realize how associated I was in this man's mind—and maybe in other people's minds as well—with drinking.

I had him bring a glass of club soda instead, so when the people came on the boat for the event, that's what I was drinking. And that's what I drank the whole night. It was tough. I drank so much club soda that evening, but I had the willpower to go at least one night without a drink. The next night I did have a drink, but much less than I was used to. I was able to see that I could control my drinking, and that I should control it. Ever since then, I have done so. A lot has to do with my being a control freak. I've always been a bit of a nut on that subject. My own self-image would not allow me to accept that my drinking, or my need for a drink, controlled me. If a strong man, as Ben Zoma taught, is one who controls his inclinations, then I had to assert my strength and bring my drinking under control.*

As these few examples make clear, even though I have long had real problems with the idea that there is a God who acts in this world and in people's lives, I have not had similar doubts about the value of Torah or of Jewish teachings. When I go to synagogue, I might have trouble believing that God will respond to my prayers or, for that matter, even cares whether or not I pray, but I have no trouble sitting in synagogue during the service, reading the Torah and its commentaries, and thinking about how to apply them to my life.

Other aspects of the Jewish tradition—most importantly, the idea that we Jews are a people—have always appealed to me. Quite simply, it's an issue of both pride and enjoyment. When I look around and see the contributions that the Jewish people have made to society, both individually and collectively, I am very pleased. The fact that we Jews make up about one-fifth of 1 percent of the world's population, roughly two people out of every thousand, and routinely win some 20 per-

---

* I've worked on issues of self-control throughout my life. I used to be a good swimmer, and then, at seventeen, I started smoking. A few months later, during the summer, a friend challenged me to race in a swimming pool. It should have been easy for me, but when I got out of the pool, I could barely stand up and I felt totally winded. I thought, *Smoking has got to be bad for you.* After that, I never smoked again.

cent of the Nobel Prizes, and do so decade after decade, cannot be dismissed as mere coincidence. It is due, at least in part—and I think in large part—to the fact that the Jewish tradition, from its earliest days, has made study an obligation. The Torah itself commands, "And you shall teach your children" (Deuteronomy 6:7). The Talmud ruled two thousand years ago that the Jewish community has to establish a school system in every city and that everyone, including the poor, must be given access to it. One of the things former president Bill Clinton wrote about in his recent book on charity (*Giving: How Each of Us Can Change the World*, New York: Knopf, 2007) is that over a hundred million children today throughout the world do not receive any education at all. That's very distressing, because what sort of future—other than one of terrible poverty—are such children going to have? So when I look at the overrepresentation of Jews in the world's intellectual development, I realize that it comes out of a tradition that regards study as a holy endeavor.

It's not just the achievements of individual Jews of which I am proud. It is the signal achievements of the Jewish people, who brought the idea of God to the world, and who brought to the world the Torah and the belief that all human beings were created by God. Which means that all of us are created equal. Racists argue that members of their race are superior to those of other races, an idea flatly denied by the Torah. According to the Torah, humanity began with God's creation of Adam and Eve, from whom we are all descended. Based on this teaching, the Talmud holds that the reason the Bible traces our descent from the same couple is "for the sake of peace among people, so that no one should say to his fellow, 'My father is greater than your father.'" The idea that God is the father of each of us, and that we therefore are all brothers and sisters and have equal value as creatures created in God's image, is about the greatest ideal in all the world. I'm very pleased to be a member of the people who brought this idea to the world.

But for me it's much more than just pride in being Jewish: I also enjoy being with fellow Jews and being part of the Jewish community. The truth is, I'm a people person, and anything that creates a sense of community appeals to me. For that matter, I love people who come from Long Beach. When I meet people who do, particularly if they grew up there around the time I did, I feel an immediate attachment to them. I love the whole idea of Long Beach—the rich interrelationships that existed there when I was a kid. Community is an important part of my life. A few years ago, I tried to start a new business, Energy 1, a company designed to market candy bars filled with vitamins. I think the idea is a viable one, but I eventually realized that, at age eighty, I didn't have the commitment to put in the hours necessary to launch such a company. Yet, when I thought about what was motivating me to suddenly start a new company, I realized that I missed being part of a community. I like having a group of people to work with. Now, instead of trying to create new business ventures, over these past years I have devoted myself to developing an Orthodox synagogue, the New Synagogue of Palm Beach. I love having a place to go to

Friday night and Saturday morning. I know it might sound funny—with all the doubts I harbor about the effects of prayers on God—but I like to sit in *shul* (the Yiddish word for synagogue) and read through the prayers, and I like doing so among friends. Someone told me that the late Jewish writer Harry Golden said that his father, who was not particularly religious, used to go to synagogue every Shabbat. So Golden said to him, "Why do you go if you have so many doubts about all that stuff?" His father answered: "You know my friend Sam? Sam goes to *shul* to speak to God. I go to *shul* to speak to Sam."

I suppose I do both. For all my questions, I've prayed a lot in my life. As a matter of fact, until my late fifties, I put on tefillin every weekday morning (tefillin are not worn on the Sabbath and most holidays), and when my son reaches his Bar Mitzvah, I certainly will want to teach him how to do so. Just as I've taught my children to say the Sh'ma. Each night, before Sarah goes to sleep, I go into her room. It could be late, and I'll tell her it's time to turn off the TV or the movie. She'll say, "Ah, don't turn it off. I don't want to go to sleep. It's boring. I want to stay awake." And I'll say, "Come on, Sarah. It's time to say the *Sh'ma*." And she'll say it, "*Sh'ma Yisrael...*" Then I'll start reciting the paragraph that follows, "*Ve'ahavta...*—And you shall love the Lord your God with all your heart, with all your soul, and with all your might...." And she repeats it as I say it. As she's saying it, she starts yawning, and when she finishes those few sentences, she's asleep. In three minutes. I think it's so good to go to sleep with the words of the Sh'ma as the final words of the day.

Though many people think of Judaism primarily as a religion, the sense of community is every bit as central to Judaism as the belief in God. When Ruth, the first convert described in the Bible, decides that she wants to become a Jew, she says to her Jewish mother-in-law, Naomi, "Your people are my people, your God is my God." To me, it's significant that she mentions her desire to join the Jewish people even before she mentions her desire to accept the Jewish God. I believe that this feeling of community is natural, not just to human beings, but to all creatures. "Birds of a feather flock together," we like to say, just as fish swim together in a school. People enjoy living in an environment with other people with whom they feel a connection. Love that reaches beyond our immediate family comes from the joy of being together with others who share our values, and who love the things we love.

The Jewish notion of community extends to all Jews, including those who live in other countries. That's why I care so passionately about helping to bring peace to Israel. I worry about Israel, because I am a Jew and I'm devoted to the Jewish community. And I want Israel to pursue policies that are wise and will lead to peace with the Arab world.

AFFECTING HOW NON-JEWS THINK ABOUT JEWS

Fifty, and certainly a hundred, years ago, being Jewish was a very difficult burden to carry. Today, in a society like the United States, being Jewish has a very strong positive connotation. Why is it that so many

Jews today have such a good feeling about themselves and why do non-Jews have a much more positive feeling about Jews than they did in the past? As far as I can see, it's not because of the religion or the religious rituals. I have never heard a non-Jew say that he admires Jews because Jewish men put on *tefillin* in the morning, and keep the laws of Shabbat. It's because of values associated with the Jewish community, values such as education, and the fact that Jews promote education in every society in which they live. Non-Jews, by and large, are impressed to learn that while Jews make up only a small proportion of the American population they comprise about 20 percent of the students at America's Ivy League colleges and an even greater percentage of the faculty. And Jews are admired for being devoted to their families. It's no coincidence that the most famous of the Ten Commandments (the most influential legal document in the Torah) is "Honor your father and mother." Jews are also associated with charitable giving.

Also, it's always been important to me that people associate me and my Jewishness with fairness. When I sold Slim-Fast, I made the decision to give every employee of the company a full year's salary as a bonus. I didn't want people thinking, let alone saying, "That son-of-a-bitch—I worked hard for him, and he takes all the money." I wanted to make the day of the sale a day of celebration for everyone. People who had been with Slim-Fast for a long time got bigger bonuses. I want people to associate me, and to associate Jews, with these sorts of noble values—generosity and fairness in business. Not just because I think these values will cause people to admire and like Jews, but because I think these values are characteristic Jewish values. For thousands of years, anti-Semites poisoned people's minds and caused them to think that Jews despised non-Jews, that Jews are the sort of people depicted in Shakespeare's *Merchant of Venice*, who will take a pound of flesh from a man who can't repay a loan, and that Jews are even involved in a conspiracy to rule the world. These hateful images have caused Jews to be victims of terrible violence and assaults, culminating in the Holocaust. It is one of my passions to make known to the world all the good things the Jews have done, most notably that we are the people who introduced the commandment to "Love your neighbor as yourself" (Leviticus 19:18) to humanity.

I'm proud to be a member of the people who brought this teaching—and so many others—to the world.

XII

⮜⮞

16 Life Lessons
Learned along the Way

1. NEVER, NEVER, NEVER GIVE UP.

One of the most difficult experiences of my life occurred when Rebecca, my first child, was born. Normally, this is a time of the greatest joy, but shortly after Rebecca's birth the doctors detected serious heart problems. They soon diagnosed her condition as Total Anomalous Pulmonary Venous Return (TAPVR). In a healthy, normally functioning heart, the pulmonary veins—two on each side—return oxygen-rich blood from the lungs to the left atrium of the heart. In patients with this very rare congenital disease, the four pulmonary veins do not connect to the left atrium (in other words, to the left side of the heart).* While there

---

* In medical terms, Total Anomalous Pulmonary Venous Return (TAPVR) is a rare congenital malformation in which the four pulmonary veins don't connect normally to the left atrium, but instead drain abnormally into the right atrium by way of an abnormal (anomalous) connection.

have been great advances in the treatment of this condition over the past decades, in 1964, when Rebecca was born, TAPVR was almost always fatal. Indeed, that's what they told me at the hospital. The doctors connected me to a doctor, the only one they knew who treated this condition, and I questioned him carefully. He described the procedure by which he would try to correct the abnormality. After he finished his description, I asked him a question that had been suggested to me by my friend, Dr. Saul Heller: "How many of the patients you've performed this operation on were alive thirty days later?" He answered, "None."

At that point, I cried. I rarely cry. As I noted earlier (see page 95), I'm not normally a highly emotional guy, and I was raised at a time in American life when men did not show their emotions easily. I can probably count on the fingers of one hand the number of times I have cried. But this time I cried. I was already forty, and here was Rebecca, my first child, born with a condition that could kill her, and everyone around me was telling me the case was hopeless.

I couldn't accept that. I kept asking myself, *How could I find out who the best doctor was even though I wasn't connected with the medical hierarchy? How could I find the best doctor to at least look at Rebecca, and maybe offer a prognosis unavailable at the hospital where she was, and unknown to the doctor to whom I had been sent?* A thought came to me. I sat down and typed out letters, and sent one to every senator and to every member of the House of Representatives. I briefly described Rebecca's condition, and asked these senators and members of Congress if they knew of any doctors in their district or state or anywhere else who they thought I should consult. Over five hundred letters went out, and three responses came back. Unfortunately, I don't recall the name of the third respondent, but the other two were New York's Senator Jacob Javits, and the newly elected young senator from Massachusetts, Ted Kennedy. Both Javits and Kennedy each sent back the names of five doctors. What struck me was that one name—Dr. John Kirklin—appeared on both lists.

I called him. He was a highly regarded heart surgeon, and a busy man. He was also very kind. I told him that I had been referred to him by Senators Javits and Kennedy. Dr. Kirklin told me to send him the papers on Rebecca's *workup*. That was the word he used. I sent all the papers along, and when I called him a few days later, he said, "Yes, I see this. I can do it. No surgery is without risk, but in my hands I really believe it's no more risky than an appendicitis operation." I must confess that his words made me cry again. I mean all this came after we had been told—and told often—that there was no hope.

As soon as the operation was over, Dr. Kirklin came into the waiting room, where I was standing with my wife Estanne (many years later, we divorced). You can imagine how nervous we were. He immediately put us at ease. "Well, I found what I expected to find, I did what I expected to do, and she's fine." I was just so overwhelmed. The two of us started showering him with gratitude. "Don't thank me," he responded. "I can only do what man can do."

I'll never forget those words. I stayed in touch with Dr. Kirklin, and every year, around the time of Rebecca's birthday, I would send him pictures of her. Years later, when Rebecca married and moved to Israel, I arranged for him to travel to Israel and speak at the major Israeli hospitals on heart surgery. These hospitals were honored to host him. By that time, Dr. Kirklin was world-renowned for refining the heart-lung machine to the point where heart surgeries could be performed with a high degree of success. In fact, he is widely acknowledged as the man who brought the heart-lung machine into routine use in heart surgery. In later years, Dr. Kirklin became chair of the Department of Surgery at the University of Alabama School of Medicine and helped develop the university's hospital system into one of the leaders in the health-care industry.

I learned a lot from this episode. If the first experts you consult tell you that nothing can be done, find other experts, particularly when the stakes are the life and death of your child. The first people I consulted had goodwill, but they simply didn't know enough. Kirklin thought outside the box, and came up with a new way of operating in such cases. It still gives me shudders to think that if I hadn't written those letters, and if the people working in Senator Javits's and Kennedy's office hadn't taken the time to research the matter and write back to me, I could have lost my daughter.

There's a famous line of Winston Churchill's. It was during the middle of World War II, and it was by no means clear yet that the Allies would win the war. One day, Churchill took the time to visit Harrow, the school he had attended as a boy. While there, Churchill, Harrow's most famous graduate, gave the students their lesson for the day: "Never give in, never give in, never,

never, never, never. . . . Never yield to the apparently overwhelming might of the enemy." In our case, the enemy was not a foreign foe, but a deadly bodily malfunction. And thank God we didn't give in, and were able to correct it.

MY FIRST BOOK

Ironically, because of a hole in Rebecca's heart, we were able to postpone the operation until she was four. I knew it would be frightening for her to be in a hospital and to have this procedure done, so in preparation for the operation I wrote a short book about a little girl born with a hole in her heart that had to be fixed. She went to the doctor, who sat her on his lap and explained that he had to sew up the hole. The girl went to a hospital with her mommy and daddy and her dolls, and was then brought to the room where the doctor could sew up the hole. After the operation, the little girl got all better. When she grew up, she married a handsome prince, and they had a baby and named the girl Rebecca.

After writing the story, I had it illustrated by my friend Paul Craniotes, and we printed one copy. Thank goodness for that book. When we went to the hospital, Rebecca was relatively calm and the entire procedure went without undue trauma.

2. I NEVER SAW A MAN PICK A FIGHT WITH A STRONGER MAN.

I recall an incident that happened to me during the festival of Sukkot. On this holiday, celebrating the fall harvest, Jews build small booths and eat their meals

inside them for seven days. At the time—it was in the
early 1960s—I was living in a Manhattan apartment on
Second Avenue and 86th Street. I had just come home
from synagogue and had walked up eighteen flights of
stairs to my apartment. In those days, I strictly observed the Jewish law forbidding the use of electricity
and therefore elevators on the Sabbath and holidays, a
law that was enacted long before elevators and buildings with eighteen floors were built. Anyway, I finally
made it upstairs, and went out to the terrace to cool
off. Pretty soon I heard a loud voice from the street.
The speaker was talking into a loudspeaker, and I
heard him referring to the well-known Jewish senator
from New York, Jacob Javits. Only he was calling him
"Jakie Javits," and throwing in disgusting comments
about "niggers."

It was a little hard for me to believe this was happening in the early 1960s on New York's Upper East
Side, an upscale neighborhood. I had been studying
karate; because of the long terrible history of anti-
Semitism, I believed it was important for Jews to be
strong and capable of defending themselves. I was curi-
ous, so I walked down the eighteen floors I had just
walked up to see what was going on.

It was cold and drizzling on the street. I walked
over to the corner and there were a lot of cops standing
there. I asked one of them, "What's going on?" and he
told me, "It's an American Renaissance Party rally."
The Renaissance Party was a neo-Nazi group, which,
fortunately, doesn't exist anymore. The police officer
directed me to the other side of the street, away from
the rally. I remember thinking, "Why does he want me

to go across the street? I'm going to go over to where the speaker is." I walked over, and listened to some of his racist diatribes. I put my hands to my mouth to make a sort of impromptu megaphone, and I called out, "You Nazi bastard, go back to Germany. That's where you belong. Go join Hitler. He's six feet under and you should be with him. Where were you during the war, you bastard?"

I realized immediately that I had seriously misjudged things. I somehow thought a lot of the people in the crowd would agree with me—how could they agree with him?—but I was wrong. The next thing I knew, a group of young men was forming a semicircle around me. At least I was able to get my back against a car, so that no one could come up behind me.

They were shouting at me, and I was shouting back at them. I put my hands down in a karate stance, and confronted them, and they didn't come at me. After a few minutes of cursing at each other, I said to them, "I'm not going to waste any more time with you bastards." I backed away from them, crossing the street while walking backwards, and watching them all the time. I ended up in front of a local grocery store. There were two guys standing there. It never occurred to me that these two men might be sympathetic to the rally, but they were. One of them, who had observed my actions, started saying, "You deserved that." And I said, "You're right. I should have had fifty of my guys with me, and we would have wiped the streets with these bastards." He said, "You Jews cheat everybody. Your Jew stores charge too much for everything, cigarettes, everything." He even pointed at a nearby store that was owned by a Jew. This was the last thing I was in the mood to hear. So I said, "Why don't you go buy in a Nazi store if they charge less? Yeah, why are you worried about what the Jew stores charge? Go find a Nazi store." He turned to the guy standing next to him, a much bigger guy, and said, "Hans, hit him." I looked at the big guy and said, "Yeah, Hans, hit me." Then Hans stepped forward and took a poke at me, and I gave him a karate block, a hard shot with my arm, and he reeled back in pain. So the guy said, "Hans, hit him again." And I looked right at Hans, and I said, "Yeah, Hans, hit me again." And Hans turned and walked away.

The bottom line is that people don't attack people who are strong enough to act in their own defense. No one, no matter how strong, picks a fight with someone who is stronger. And this doesn't only apply to personal life, but to the life of nations as well.

When the Arab nations thought they could defeat and destroy Israel—and they thought so three times, in 1948, in 1967, and in 1973—they attacked Israel. Israel rebuffed the attacks all three times, coming out with far more territory (from the first two wars) than they had before the conflicts. But after the 1973 surprise attack on Israel by Egypt and Syria failed (after some early success), Egyptian president Anwar Sadat concluded that the Arab/Israeli conflict could not be decided militarily; Israel was simply too strong to be defeated on the battlefield. So what did he do? He waited a few years, came to Jerusalem, and, standing in front of the Israeli Knesset, offered to sign a full and formal peace treaty with Israel in return for the Egyptian land captured by Israel in 1967. And a short time later, Prime

Minister Menachem Begin, the great Israeli hawk, returned every inch of the Sinai. Israel and Egypt have
lived in peace ever since.

Some people complain that the peace between the
two countries has been a cold one. That's true, and it
likely will remain a cold peace until Israel reaches an
accommodation with the Palestinians and a Palestinian
state exists alongside Israel. But that is beside the
point. Because a cold peace, with no one dying, is a lot
better than a hot war. Just ask the parents of the thousands of Israelis killed in the 1948, 1967, and 1973 wars.

Israel needs to be stronger than all the nations surrounding her, combined. Any Jew who doesn't
understand that has not learned a fundamental—perhaps the most fundamental—lesson of the Holocaust.
As Rabbi Irving "Yitz" Greenberg, one of the great
thinkers in Jewish life today, has put it: "Jews must
never again be so weak that their very weakness tempts
enemies to attack them."

As I said, whether it applies to a bully like Hans and
his friend or, for that matter, to a bullying nation, I have
never seen a man pick a fight with a man stronger than
himself.

3. IF YOU WANT TO LIVE IN PEACE, MAKE SURE THAT YOU'RE STRONG.

This thought is not original, but comes straight out
of the Bible, in a verse that has probably influenced the
way I see the world almost as much as the biblical
verse, "Love your neighbor as yourself" (Leviticus
19:18). The verse comes from Psalms: "The Lord will
give strength to his people, the Lord will bless His peo-

ple with peace" (Psalms 29:11). Religious Jews recite this verse daily, several times, because it concludes the *Birkat Hamazon*, the prayer recited after meals. The Bible's meaning is clear, and it mentions strength first because only if you're strong can you live in peace. If you're strong, others won't pick on you because they will be afraid of the reaction they will provoke. Most important, if you're strong, you will have the luxury to make peace.

The last is the main reason it's important to be strong. The goal of achieving strength is not to rule over others or to take advantage of others. The goal is to lead a life of peace, something you can only achieve if you can defend yourself against those who have malicious intentions.

4. ONE PERSON CONTROLS EVERY MAJOR DECISION IN EVERY COUNTRY AND EVERY COMPANY. TO AFFECT THE POLICIES OF A GOVERNMENT OR MAKE A DEAL WITH A COMPANY, YOU HAVE TO REACH THAT ONE PERSON.

In all my travels, I have learned that one person and one person only controls every major decision in every country (including America). One person. One person has the bully pulpit and he is the leader of the country because he has the verbal powers, the capacity to use that pulpit to make speeches, and to surround himself with people who support him. He also controls the security forces.

It was this understanding of the decision-making power of the one leader that deeply influenced how I went about trying to bring peace between Israel and her neighbors. For example, I knew that if I spoke to a hundred Syrians and convinced them of the desirability of achieving peace with Israel, it would achieve no good unless one of those hundred people was Hafez Assad, Syria's president. On the other hand, if the only Syrian I persuaded to make peace was Assad, that would be enough, because he could make it happen. The day before Anwar Sadat announced his willingness to go to Israel and negotiate a peace settlement, I'm sure a poll of Egyptians would have revealed that only a few wanted to see Egypt enter into such negotiations. But once Sadat went to Israel, received a tumultuous welcome there, and made it known that he was serious about negotiating a treaty with Israel, millions of Egyptians were influenced to support such negotiations. All this came about because of the determination of one man. Reach that one man and you can make something happen.

That's why I support starting negotiations at the top level. Surprisingly, or maybe not surprisingly, most diplomats and other government officials oppose this idea. I used to plead with Syrian Foreign Minister Faruq Al-Shara to let Israeli Prime Minister Shimon Peres and President Assad get into a room together and talk. He was always opposed to that. He argued that it was better to first have lower-level diplomats and government officials meet to resolve the basic issues, and only when all the issues had been pretty much worked out to get the leaders together. Lower-level officials are unlikely to approve the compromises necessary to reach peace, because they fear they will get into trouble for proposing or accepting such compromises. So they often become hard-liners and sticklers over minor details. The leaders at the top are much more aware of which issues are negotiable and which are not. That's why peace came about much more quickly when Sadat came straight to Israel and made known what he needed in order for there to be peace. And once Sadat made it known, Prime Minister Begin made just the sort of compromises (most importantly, giving back the whole Sinai desert) that no one would have predicted he would have made a year earlier.

My fantasy is that you get the two leaders who can make a deal into a room together, and they will more often than not come to an agreement. Then, they should bring in a team of lawyers (not diplomats) and tell them: "This is the agreement we're making, work out the details."

Most likely, that's how peace will eventually be made in the Middle East. One person at the top will take responsibility for making it happen, and it will happen. So if you want to influence policy, don't spend hundreds of hours trying to persuade people who themselves can't determine policy. Get to the one person who can "green-light the deal," and influence him or her. It's pretty much the only agreement that you can be sure will work out.

5. THERE IS NO SUCH THING AS A MISTAKE.

I never like the word *"mistake"* because of what that word implies; it suggests that you were stupid for taking a certain action, and should never have done it. And yet you're judging the action not on Sunday afternoon, when it happened, but on Monday morning after the game: "Oh, damn, you never should have thrown that pass! You should have run through the center, because the pass was intercepted and the interceptor ran for a touchdown." Whoa, Monday morning everything is so clear! But on Sunday afternoon, when the defensive back is coming at the quarterback to tackle him, the quarterback's got the ball and he can't see the hole in the line, so he throws to what he thinks is a good receiver. On Monday morning you call that play a "mistake." But no one, including you, yelled out to him at the time, "Don't throw the ball because it will be intercepted." If somebody had said that at the time, that person would be a hero. But saying it on Monday morning is not heroic and is definitely not helpful.

Any time you make a decision, whether in football, business, government policy, or personal life, as long as you make it on the basis of information you have at the time, you shouldn't be faulted, and you shouldn't fault yourself if things don't work out as you expected.

Over the years, I have come to believe that the word *mistake* is one of those absurdly and unfairly used words, and one that ends up intimidating and paralyzing a lot of people. After all, what is a "mistake"? An action or decision that proves at a later point not to be as successful as you would have liked, but which was made based on the best information you had at the time. Today, you have new information, and you would make a different decision. But can you really guarantee that the decisions you do make today, no matter how confident you are about them, will be successful? Every choice we make should be based on the best judgment and information available at the time we make it. If we do that, then even if it doesn't work out, that's not a mistake—that's life.

For example, Thompson Medical once put out a product called Chocolate Lover's Diet. We were sure it would succeed, because in all our research we learned that the one thing that all overweight people love is chocolate. So we figured that if we put out a low-calorie product for chocolate lovers that would enable them to still have their chocolate and their chocolate milk shake, it would be a guaranteed winner. We tried out the product in one large store, a Duane Reade on New York's East Side. We took the store's whole front display and featured Chocolate Lover's Diet from top to bottom (I always liked to test out a product in one store, to see if it could sell on its own, without advertising). We priced the product right—$4.99—put it in a very attractive can, with a sign on top of the display, "Lose weight! Chocolate Lover's Diet." A day later we came back to the store and not one can had been sold. We came back the next day, and still nothing. A week, not one can sold! So I said, "You know, this was a great idea, but it didn't work." No one was blamed because no one had done anything wrong. At that point, I just turned to the other guys, and said, "Okay, let's donate this product to the soup kitchen."

When something doesn't turn out the way we hoped, it is certainly worth analyzing what happened and why. (Even then, as in the case of Chocolate Lover's Diet, we shouldn't always assume we'll reach accurate and helpful conclusions.) And we shouldn't conduct our analysis with an attitude of blame or with the sense that we or someone else has failed. Thomas Edison performed almost 10,000 tests in his effort to develop an improved battery, and he still hadn't succeeded. Yet when a discouraged assistant said, "You must be pretty downhearted with all these failed tests," Edison responded, "Failed? We haven't failed. We have found 10,000 ways that won't work." A short time later—maybe it was test 10,001—he developed a nickel-iron alkaline battery, one that is still in use. Edison also conducted 2,000 tests before he found the right filament for the light bulb. Imagine if he had given up after 10, or 100, or even 1,000 failed experiments. As somebody once put it, "If Edison hadn't continued after all his early failures, we might still be reading by candlelight."

Say you're a boss, and one of your employees makes a decision on the basis of what seems to be reliable information, only it leads to an unfavorable result. Don't blame him and don't call it a mistake. Hold your tongue. I know that might not be easy to do, but it's the right thing to do. If you criticize your employee in such a situation, you're going to develop a staff that will be afraid to take action or make decisions, and that will end up keeping your business from innovating and growing.

This applies in all areas of life, not just business. A child raised by a parent who always finds fault will conclude that it's better not to act than to do something and be criticized. That's why it's best not to criticize others unless it's absolutely necessary. But be generous in giving credit for the positive things others do, because if people feel good about themselves, they'll be willing to take strong action when it's necessary.

One final point: When I say there are no mistakes I don't want to sound naive. Sure I've made plenty of decisions in business that didn't work out. But I have always tried not to beat myself up about it. Doing so wouldn't make me any smarter, just more fearful. Some people think fear isn't so bad because it can stop you from making poor decisions in the future. The problem is that it will stop you from making *all* decisions—the right ones, too. As Mark Twain remarked: "A cat that sits on a hot stove will learn never to sit on a hot stove again. He'll also learn never to sit on a cold stove."

6. ALWAYS REMEMBER WHO YOU WORK FOR, AND REMEMBER, IT'S NOT YOUR BOSS.

I once got together all my top people, and asked each one, "Who do you report to?" And everybody gave the obvious answer: "I report to Joe," "I report to Danny." And I said, "You're all wrong: You all report to the consumer. That's who we all work for."

7. IF IT'S NOT BROKE, YOU CAN STILL MAKE IT BETTER: THE PHILOSOPHY OF CONTINUOUS IMPROVEMENT.

I always believed it was my responsibility to make sure that the consumer always had the best possible product at the lowest possible price. That business philosophy ensures success, continuity, and repeat sales to consumers who try your product. If consumers feel you're giving them the best product that can be made, and are offering it to them at the lowest possible price, they're going to buy again and again. Why would they go elsewhere? To buy an inferior product for more money? But while it's easy to say you're going to offer the best possible product at the lowest possible price, in practice doing so means that you have to keep working very hard, even after you have achieved success.

I once heard it said of one of the world's great pianists that even after he achieved international renown, he still practiced seven or eight hours a day. When someone asked him why—given how highly regarded and how highly skilled he was—he didn't relax and take more time off, he answered: "If I miss a day of practice, I can feel the difference in my playing. If I miss a few days of practice, my manager will notice the difference. And if I miss a week of practice, everybody will notice." What that pianist said applies to many— probably most—areas of life. That's why I always continued working on our products, even after they came out and were selling well. There's a common truism in business, "If it's not broken, don't fix it." But the bigger truth is that even if something is not broken, it's not going to run forever, and it's a lot better to work on improving it while it's still working fine and not yet broken. That's why, even when Slim-Fast came out in a can and was selling very well, I remained obsessed with improving its nutrition and its taste, even at a time when consumers thought the drink was already very nutritious and tasted good.

Another reason I kept working on it was my own sense of integrity. I have never been able to sell anything that I don't believe in. Unless I know that I'm giving the consumer the best product, I just can't sell it effectively. I'd feel like a fraud. In addition, it's not just a question of integrity. It's a matter of good business practice as well. Because if you don't keep working on improving your product, a process we called "continuous improvement" (see pages 132-133), somebody else will. If your product is selling well, and people are saying there's nothing like it, you can be sure that there will be lots of competitors thinking of ways they can improve on your product, and seduce away many of the customers.

Maybe that explains an aspect of my character that others might regard as obsessive, even neurotic, but which to me makes perfect sense. No matter how successful my business was, I always felt insecure about it; I always knew that profits could fall to zero very quickly. Does that sound paranoid to you? Who knows—maybe a little paranoia is a good thing. It keeps you working hard, so you keep building on whatever success you have.

This is true for every product, and every company. Consider General Motors, the once-textbook example of a well-run company. Its management techniques were so highly touted that they were studied in the top business schools. Had somebody told you in the 1960s that this corporation—which for many years was among the highest-earning companies in the United States—would come into the twenty-first century laying off tens of thousands of workers, facing a market share lower than the Japanese company Toyota, and eventually declaring bankruptcy, the person making those predictions would not have sounded like a prophet, but a lunatic. General Motors failed to keep challenging itself and improving its products. This is true of other major companies as well, some of which have actually disappeared. To cite just one example of GM's self-defeating practices: The company continued to produce gas-guzzling cars even after it became apparent that producing cars that used fuel more efficiently was not only the responsible thing to do, it was also the smart thing to do. But GM's executives weren't worried that there was somebody out there producing the sort of cars that would sell better in the future; they were just concerned about their current market share. As a result, they ended up losing a good part of both their present and future market share.

This has always been my philosophy. If your product is working well, keep working on making it even better. The better the product you offer consumers, the more consumers are going to trust you and stay loyal. And if you don't earn the customers' trust and loyalty, they will eventually treat you with the same disregard with which you treat them.

8. IF YOU HAVE A THEORY AND THE FACTS CONTRADICT IT, DROP YOUR THEORY.

I mentioned before that during my early years at Thompson Medical, I was selling San-Cura, Gas-Tabs, and Throat-Aid to pharmacies in New York, and using my window signs to advertise them. Suddenly, I had a competitor, another fellow posting window ads (he had learned the technique from me) for a product called Special Formula Gum, a chewing gum that supposedly helped people lose weight. Before I knew it, my pharmacist friends were telling me how well this new gum was selling, and they kept urging me to bring out a similar product. I told them no. I was sure the product was a fad. How could a little piece of chewing gum help a big, overweight person lose weight? I've always felt it was morally wrong to sell something to people that won't work, and it's also financially stupid; people will buy such a product once, and never again. So that was my theory, which I clung to with total conviction and passion: This product is pointless, it's a fad, and the company producing it will likely go out of business— probably sooner rather than later.

Then I learned something very surprising. My pharmacist friends told me the same people were coming back and buying the product again and again. That staggered me. I know enough about advertising to realize that a smart campaign can influence many people to go into a store and buy something once, particularly if it's not an expensive product. So I asked the pharmacists if they were seeing repeat sales. And they told me, "People say it works, and they keep coming back for more."

At that point, I figured I'd better look into this. Maybe Dan Abraham is sure this gum can't help people to lose weight. But maybe Dan Abraham is wrong and all the repeat purchasers are right. So I checked into the matter further, and developed Slim-Mint Gum (see pages 79–84), by far my most successful product up to that point.

Had I been unwilling to abandon my theory, I would have lost out on a lot more than Slim-Mint Gum. Because that was the product that got me into the whole world of weight loss, the area in which I've achieved my greatest business successes.

The importance of dropping a theory when it's contradicted by the facts applies in all areas of life. From the 1940s, when Israel was created, until late in the 1980s, I was convinced that the Arab world uniformly rejected Israel's right to exist and had but one ambition—to destroy Israel and drive her citizens into the sea. Thinking as I did, all I wanted was for Israel to be militarily strong and make no concessions to Arab countries, since they would merely utilize any concessions to harm Israel.

Then, in 1988, I started traveling with Congressman Wayne Owens (D-Utah) to meet with both Arab and Israeli leaders. I soon learned that there were high-level Arab leaders, such as Hosni Mubarak, the president of Egypt, who wanted to see Israel negotiate peace settlements with all the countries in the Arab world (Israel had already negotiated a peace treaty with Egypt in 1978). Even hard-line Arab leaders, like President Hafez Assad of Syria, expressed to me a willingness to enter into peaceful relations with Israel as long as Syria received in return the Golan Heights, the land Syria had lost to Israel in the Six-Day War.* So I changed my theory, and have devoted a good part of my life ever since to trying to bring Arab and Israeli leaders together in an environment that can lead to a just, comprehensive, and permanent peace.

If I had not been willing to change my theories when confronted with new information, I would never have achieved anywhere near the business success that

---

* I passed on the contents of my meeting with Assad to Prime Minister Benjamin Netanyahu (then serving his first term as prime minister, 1996–1999). See the discussion of this episode in my book *Peace Is Possible* (New York: Newmarket, 2006), pages 123–129.

I have had, and I would be locked into a hopeless and depressed belief that Israelis will have to go on fighting wars for generation after generation. Such a belief is not only tragic, it is wrong, and if enough people come to understand that it is wrong, we will have peace in the Middle East very soon. Israel must, for its own future, make the strategic decision that peace with the Arab world is in its best interest.

That's why it's fine to have theories about different things, but only if you're willing to change them when they no longer accord with the facts.

9. THE LAST QUESTION I ASK IN A NEGOTIATION.

I think back to the many times in a negotiation with one of our suppliers when there would be a vigorous give-and-take. It could be on some small item. My opposite number would be asking $10 a thousand, I'd be offering $7, and we'd end up settling, let's say, for $8. Then, we'd agree, we'd shake hands, but I would say to him: "Are you making a profit at this price?" And if he said, "No," I'd tell him, "I don't want to do that to you. Tell me what you need to make a profit."

I never wanted someone who was dealing with me to lose money, particularly since I was going to be using the product he was supplying. There's something very wrong with bargaining with someone to the point that he or she would sell it to you at a loss, or at no profit. It's not just that I'm a considerate person who tries to be fair. It's a matter of good business practice as well. If he doesn't make money, he's not going to survive. And then I will have lost a good supplier.

Greedy behavior is not just an ugly character trait; it is also the wrong thing businesswise as well.

It was always true that for a business deal to be a success it had to be win-win, for the supplier (or the customer) and for me as well. Certainly, we could argue vigorously in the negotiations. I didn't want to get taken advantage of. But at the end of the day, I wanted that supplier or customer to want to keep working with me, to feel that if he worked with me he'd make money and be treated fairly. Many, if not most, people think that businesspeople have to be ruthless (I don't think that way at all). Businesspeople are people who happen to do business. No matter what they do, people—writers, lawyers, doctors, nurses—are people first, and their first obligation is to live like civilized and caring human beings. Ruthless people, on the other hand, assume that in every transaction there's a winner and a loser, and their whole mind-set is focused on making sure they're not the loser. Would you want to deal with a person like that? Of course not. Why would I want to be the sort of person people would dread dealing with, when usually there is enough on the table for all parties to come out satisfied?

10. Being prudent is not always prudent.

For a number of years, Slim-Fast achieved such success that people forgot how much competition we had at first. I remember that American Home Products had a division called Lederle Labs, and they brought out a product called Dynatrim, which I feared might give us a real run for our money. But Dynatrim didn't last. The product that really concerned me was something Nestlé put out called Sweet Success. Like American Home Products, Nestlé is a giant company, and the name that Nestlé gave its product, Sweet Success, was attractive, but what really frightened me were reports I was hearing from California. In test-marketing in a limited area, Sweet Success was getting up to 50 percent of the market share. We were doing well at the time, but I remember the thought that went through my mind: *50 percent, wow! It looks like they're going to be tough competition.* So we carefully checked out all their advertising, and the first thing that struck us was that their entire focus was on taste. Not a lot there about health and weight loss, but a big spotlight on taste. They were really coming after us.

We immediately launched a new national advertising campaign for Slim-Fast, this time focusing on how good it tasted. By the time Sweet Success' executives launched their national campaign with the emphasis on taste, we had preempted theirs with our campaign on how delicious Slim-Fast tasted.

I learned a lot from that incident, and not just the obvious lesson—that if your competitor has developed a successful technique, don't fight it, but learn from it. I also learned something else. Being prudent is not always prudent. Obviously, it seemed safe to Nestlé executives to test-market their product very carefully before putting in the money to launch it nationally. But in this case, their prudence cost them. Had Nestlé gone national with Sweet Success before the company went into a test market, I don't know how effectively we would have been able to promote Slim-Fast as the great-tasting product.

11. PUT YOUR PROBLEMS ON THE TABLE.

Many employees in a business keep quiet when they start seeing a problem, even more so if they think they've caused it. They're afraid they'll get in trouble if they reveal what's going on, so they convince themselves that they're going to correct the problem on their own. Or they're afraid to be the bearer of bad tidings. This can cause catastrophic results.

In recent years, there have been instances in which large investment banks and brokerage houses have been threatened with bankruptcy because an employee ran up billions of dollars in trading losses in an effort to turn around losses that had at first amounted to much less.

When something is going wrong, put it on the table. When five people with wide experience put their heads together, they are far more likely to come up with a workable solution than a lone individual who is already frightened and nervous, possibly even desperate. Imagine if those desperate traders had come in to their bosses when they were down $20 million, instead of billions.

I like to tell people, "Put it on the table, because we all eat from the same table." Or, as my friend Moe Ratowsky—one of the very first employees of our company—used to say, "Don't hide a problem. Once you know you have a problem, you don't have the problem anymore."

12. THERE ARE TIMES WHEN MAKING A DECISION ON THE BASIS OF INSTINCT ALONE IS THE ONLY REASONABLE THING TO DO.

We used to do consumer research by asking people, for example, "Which of these two packages do you like better—this one or that one?" The only difference was the color—one was blue, one red. Everything else on the package was the same—the typeface, the copy, everything. I didn't tell the people whose opinions we asked that the only difference between the packages was the color. I simply asked, "Which package do you like better?" I noticed that if you broadened the question, asking them why they preferred one package over the other, you'd never get the true answer. All I needed to find out was how many people liked this package and how many people liked that one. And I was totally willing to go with the consensus. There are times when 'why' doesn't matter. In many cases, people can't tell you the truth because they themselves don't know why they made the decision. They decide based on instinctive preference alone.

13. "DO YOU WANT TO BE A SCHLOCK COMPANY, WHERE EVERYONE IS GOING TO COMPETE WITH YOU ON PRICE, OR DO YOU WANT TO BE A BRAND-NAME COMPANY WITH A UNIQUE PRODUCT YOU CAN BE PROUD OF?"

There's an old Jewish proverb: "My friend is he who will tell me my faults in private." The fellow who first set down that thought was Solomon ibn Gabirol, a Jewish poet and philosopher in eleventh-century Spain. It's also one of those truisms that becomes obvious only after you hear it, but not the sort of thing you tend to think about otherwise.

Anyway, I mentioned earlier what a great, loyal friend Charlie Elson, the Walgreens buyer in Chicago, was. Even when the FDA was going after Slim-Mint Gum, Charlie made sure Walgreens kept selling it. As long as the product was legal and he believed in it and in me, he stood by me. And he stood by me during other challenges as well. At one time, I had taken in as a 10 percent partner a friend named Bill. I'll leave out the man's last name, since this is not a flattering story. At the time, Bill, who had been a close childhood friend of mine from Long Beach, bought a share in my business. Unfortunately, we later had a somewhat unhappy parting of the ways. I bought him out, and paid him back every cent he had put into the business, plus. Almost immediately after that, Bill went into competition with me, and started putting out a gum called Slim and Trim. It was a very nice-looking product. The truth is I think he had learned something about how to attractively package products during the years he had been with us. Bill, of course, knew Charlie Elson because, in the past, he had often sold Thompson Medical products to him. I found out later that he had gone to see Charlie, and had started talking very critically about me, and about Slim-Mint as well, telling Charlie how much better his Slim and Trim was. Charlie just looked him in the eye and said, "Bill, put that product back in your bag, get up and leave, and don't come back." Then he added: "If you want to sell me a product, don't tell me how bad someone else is whom I'm buying from. I'm buying from Thompson Medical

Company. You're talking badly about Danny and Thompson Medical Company, and I don't want to hear that. So just leave."

I learned a lot about ethics and integrity from Charlie, not the least of which was never to speak badly about a competitor. To this day, I also try never to speak badly about anyone. The truth is, though Charlie was an Irish Catholic, his behavior was entirely in keeping with one set of Judaism's distinctive and very significant laws, the laws of *lashon hara*, which prohibit one from speaking ill of others unless the person to whom you're speaking has a real need for the information. For example, if someone is about to go into business with a person whom you know to be dishonest, or genuinely lazy, you have the right to share that information with the involved party. But even in such a case, you shouldn't go around telling what you know to people who have no need for this information. Bill had every right to try to sell Slim and Trim, and to tell Charlie why it was the best product on the market, or even what a great deal he was willing to make with him. What he didn't have a right to do was to run me and my product down. And I was so touched that Charlie called him on it.

Charlie was more than just a loyal and highly ethical guy. He was very smart, and any time he thought I was doing something wrong, he told me. On one occasion, he might well have saved me from going down a path that could have done great damage to my career. I showed up at his office with an attaché case containing new products. I thought if we could place these products in his stores, they would sell well and generate a whole new income stream. One of them was an item we called Sleep-Aid, another was called Combat-Cold tablets. They were all well-named, nicely packaged, and intended to prompt impulse sales. There were a few other products in the case, a total of four or five, and we had worked hard to get them right. Charlie looked over the whole group, and then said to me, "Danny, put the products back in your case. Look, you have to decide: Do you want to be a schlock company, where everyone is going to compete with you on price, or do you want to be a brand-name company with a unique product you can be proud of? If you go the schlock route, I'm going to have to buy the cheapest product available."

It was one of the best pieces of advice I ever got. And I could trust it, because I knew that Charlie sincerely wished me well and wanted me to succeed. That's why, when new products came out in the realm of diet management, he would always nudge me to develop something new myself, my way, with some sort of improvement. He pushed me because he knew that I, and the people with me at Thompson Medical, knew the world of dieting, and could be innovative and produce something special. What he didn't want me and Thompson Medical to become was another bottom fisher with no distinctive identity. He was a good enough friend to tell me that. To my face. And in private.

14. WE ALL HAVE BOTH GOOD AND BAD LUCK IN OUR LIVES, BUT MANY OF US DON'T PREPARE FOR EITHER.

Luck is a tricky issue. If a person achieves a lot of success and doesn't acknowledge that any of it came from luck, he's arrogant. It's as if he's saying, "Everything I got I earned and deserved. It's all due to me and my intelligence." He doesn't even seem to allow room for God. And the truth is, luck is important. But over the years I've come to realize something else as well. A lot of people—even some of those who think of themselves as unlucky—have luck, but they don't take advantage of it. So for all practical purposes, luck has been wasted on them. You have to train for luck, and prepare for it. Because luck comes in the form of opportunities all the time, and if you're not prepared for it and you're not willing to work hard once it comes your way, you won't be able to take advantage of it.

For example, many Americans today have more money than they need (I first wrote this before the severe recession of 2008–2009 started). But instead of appreciating how lucky they are, and saving money to tide them over in less lucky days, they spend more than they need to spend and buy frivolous things. If they have a credit card, they go into debt, buying things that aren't necessities.

In my poorer years, I learned lessons that still shape my actions today. For example, you don't have to dress in the most expensive style, you can wear last year's clothes, still look pretty good, and these clothes will still keep you warm. Between the ages of twenty-four and thirty, I had one pair of shoes—that was it. I brought those shoes in to be repaired when I needed to have them fixed, and sat in the store while they were being resoled and reheeled. For six years, I was able to get by on that one pair, and didn't buy another one because, frankly, I was short on money, and what I did have I spent on bigger priorities than new shoes, like going out on dates.

Many people I know buy new clothes that they don't need, simply because it makes them feel good to do so. It's fine to buy things when you have the money to pay for them. But it's a squandering of luck to pay with a credit card, and put yourself in unnecessary debt.

This has been a guiding principle for me: Never spend more than you make. I wasn't always like this. Early in my business career, I overextended myself, and it almost destroyed me. It was certainly one of the more scary experiences of my life. In those days, we used to ship products to our customers, send them an invoice, and then wait thirty, sixty, ninety days, or more for the customers to pay.

I would then take the invoice to a special kind of banker—they were called factors, and it was a popular profession back then. The factors would give us cash for 70 to 80 percent of the receivables. So, at one point, I went to the factor I did business with, and I brought him new accounts receivable. I needed the money to meet my payroll. The factor just looked me in the eye and said he was not going to buy my notes anymore. "You're getting too many returns from your customers," he said. "I don't believe you're going to be solid, and I don't want to be stuck holding paper for goods that have been returned and that won't be paid for." I started sweating. I told him I needed the money to pay my employees and that, in any case, he certainly should have given me notice. He was unmoved by my appeal. "Shoulda, woulda, coulda," he said. "It doesn't matter. You're cut off, and we're no longer accepting the risk of your paper." When I left his office, I was very nervous. And in my nervousness, I remember thinking one thing: *I would never again go into debt.*

I could have been wiped out that day, but one of the things that saved me was an odd trait of mine. I don't believe in secretiveness. A lot of people do. They don't tell anybody anything, particularly something unpleasant or ugly, like the fact that they are desperately in need of money. My attitude is different. I believe in talking about your problems, because if you talk to enough people, you're going to come across someone who can help you solve them. So that's a principle I've always acted on. I tell people what my problems are, what my needs are, and sooner or later—and this time I needed it sooner—someone will give me an idea that will work.

So I told people I met that I was in a tough spot. Someone I knew, not even all that well, directed me to a bank that was just down the street. I walked in and started to talk to a loan officer there about my need for a line of credit, maybe up to $25,000, and before I knew it he had introduced me to the president of that branch of the bank. The man's name was Al Fader, and I outlined my problem to him. To my considerable amazement, he agreed to lend me the full $25,000.* I was so taken aback, I said to him—in retrospect, this might not have been the smartest ploy—"Why are you giving me the loan, particularly after finding out that I was cut off by the factor?" I still cherish the answer he gave me: "Because you have an honest face. We don't just examine equities and assets here. We also look at the people to whom we make loans. And we feel if they're honest, we'll get paid back."

Years later, someone told me something the British writer G. K. Chesterton had written: "We think for a landlady considering a lodger, it is important to know his income, but still more important to know his philosophy." Chesterton was right, just as that banker was right. An honest person, even if he or she is temporarily without funds, will eventually pay back their debts. A dishonest person, even if he's affluent, will find ways to cheat you.

So I was very touched when this banker told me he trusted me, and gave me the loan. But that case was an absolute necessity; without the loan I would have lost my business. Ever since, I have resolved not to spend more than I am making. The moment that ever started happening in a business, I'd put an immediate hold on all unnecessary expenses. The word went out to the sales force, for example, to drive instead of flying to see customers.

---

* I realize this sounds funny, given that I had just made up my mind to never again go into debt. But I knew that my financial survival depended on my paying my employees and paying my bills. Once I got through that, I could start cutting down on my expenses, and avoid borrowing unnecessary funds.

Remember, if you prepare yourself and don't spend unnecessarily, you will be able to take advantage of lucky opportunities that present themselves, and you'll avoid being crushed during a less lucky period.

15. "WHEN YOU'RE RIGHT AND YOU FIGHT HARD ENOUGH, YOU ALWAYS WIN."

I describe earlier (see pages 89–95) how I had to go to battle against the FDA (the Food and Drug Administration) when FDA officials tried to force me to change the name of what was, until then, my most successful product, Slim-Mint Gum, and to stop claiming that it could help people lose weight (which, in fact, it could). In the end there was a two-week trial, which Slim-Mint (part of Thompson Medical) won. It was very unusual for a small company to challenge the FDA and win, and the case garnered a lot of attention.

A few moments after the verdict was announced, I went off with my lawyer, Pat Hatry, to a small room in the courthouse. Once inside, I started crying—one of the few times in my life when I did so. I said to Pat, "If we had lost, I would have lost everything. The whole business. My entire future would have gone up in smoke in front of me." And Pat said, "Danny, when you're right and you fight hard enough, you will always win."

That was certainly one of the best pieces of advice I've ever received. It's important not to let yourself be bullied. It's terrible to be bullied, even when you're in the wrong, but it's particularly important to fight back when you're in the right. If you don't, not only do you lose your self-respect, but you also can lose your entire life's work.

16. "There's only one obligation that applies to you: 'Come home alive.'"

I've told the story of how, when I was preparing to go off to join the army to fight in World War II, my mentor and teacher, Simon Solomon, offered me the following advice: "Danny, when you're in the army, don't worry about Shabbes [that's the Eastern European pronunciation], don't worry about tefillin, don't worry about keeping kosher. There's only one obligation that applies to you now: 'Come home alive.'"

Most fundamentally, Mr. Solomon was telling me to keep my priorities in order. And at the top of the list was staying alive (obviously, that's not always something a soldier has control over; Mr. Solomon just meant that I shouldn't take foolish risks or needlessly endanger myself).

Mr. Solomon was a highly religious Jew and his advice (though some religious Jews would have put greater emphasis on observing Jewish rituals, even in the difficult setting of the army) epitomized for me one of the reasons I love Judaism so much. It's practical, it's ethical, and it embodies a love of life. Ask religious Jews what the goal of their life should be and they will generally answer, "To do God's will." But to do that, as Mr. Solomon knew, you have to be alive. As the Psalms teach, "The dead cannot praise God" (Psalms 115:17). Mr. Solomon understood that I would have many years in which to pray, keep kosher, and observe Shabbat, but all that depended on one thing: staying alive.

Which leads me to the biggest lesson of all: The purpose of life is . . . to live; to love; to do good; and to be happy. L'Chaim! To life!

ACKNOWLEDGMENTS

I would like to thank Rabbi Joseph Telushkin, who worked carefully with me to turn the events and lessons of my life into a readable narrative that I hope can teach and touch you, my reader.

Index

About the Author

S. Daniel Abraham, a leading American entrepreneur and pioneer in both the pharmaceutical and diet food business, is the creator of Slim-Fast Foods, the most successful diet product in history. A World War II infantry veteran, Mr. Abraham's business career began with the acquisition of Thompson Medical Company Inc. in 1947. A philanthropist, Abraham is dedicated to a variety of causes, among them improving health care and nutrition, encouraging Middle East peace, and broadening educational opportunities. His gift to the Mayo Clinic served to create the highly innovative Dan Abraham Healthy Living Center, whose opening in 2007 received national media coverage.

Abraham is the founder of the Center for Middle Peace and Economic Cooperation in Washington, D.C. He is a close friend of many top leaders in the United States, Israel, and throughout the Arab world, and through those personal channels has worked tirelessly over the past two decades to help bring an end to the

Arab/Israeli conflict. He is a major sponsor of the Washington-based United States Institute of Peace.

A passionate advocate and supporter of higher education, Abraham has endowed an S. Daniel Abraham Chair in Middle East Policy Studies at Princeton University, and a Chair in Nutritional Medicine at Harvard University Medical School. He has also funded the Dan Abraham School for Business Administration and Economics at Bar-Ilan University in Israel, the S. Daniel Abraham Israel Program at Yeshiva University, and the S. Daniel Abraham Honors Program at Stern College for Women. He holds honorary doctorates from Ben-Gurion University, Bar-Ilan University, and Yeshiva University. He is also the founder of the New Synagogue of Palm Beach.

Mr. Abraham and his wife, Ewa, reside in Palm Beach with their daughter Sarah and son Sam. He also has four grown daughters, Rebecca, Leah, Tammy, and Simmy, twenty-six grandchildren, and three great-grandchildren.

Addendum

REMINISCENCES ABOUT DAN ON THE OCCASION OF HIS EIGHTIETH BIRTHDAY

In 2004, on the occasion of Daniel Abraham's eightieth birthday, his daughter Simmy contacted many of his relatives, friends, and lifelong business associates and asked them to write birthday letters to her father. She specifically asked the participants, all of whom had known Dan for many years—some for decades—to include the sort of telling anecdotes that capture her father's spirit.

In 2009, in Dan's eighty-fifth birthday year, as he was completing work on his autobiography, *Everything Is Possible: Life and Business Lessons from a Self-Made Billionaire and the Founder of Slim-Fast* (published by Newmarket Press), his rightfully proud family urged him to make public some of these wonderful tributes. Hence a number of these recollections are excerpted in this Addendum and published in this Special Edition of Dan's book. Contributors are Bill Clinton, Shimon Peres, Aura Herzog, Isaac Herzog, Madeline Albright, Sandy Berger, Rahm Emanuel, H. Douglas Owens, Dan Rothem, Jihan "Gigi" Ghanim, Moses Ratowsky, Dan Horwitz, Tom Kemeny, Charles Noonan, Carl T. Tsang, Monty Marsala, Tim McCain, Stephen Novick, Samuel Heyman, James Katzman, Rabbi Kenneth Brander, Rabbi Haskel Lookstein, Rabbi Shlomo Riskin, Rabbi Avi Weiss, Rabbi Moshe Rom, David Altman, Jim Hodge, and daughters Simmy, Tammy, Leah, and Rebecca.

From Former U.S. President
William Jefferson Clinton

WILLIAM JEFFERSON CLINTON

Dear Danny,

Although the pool of such people is growing alarmingly small, I always try to learn something from those who have a few years on me. With you, there is no shortage of things to learn: the importance of persistence, of friendship, of believing in others, of working hard and dreaming big, and of strength and spirit. Your years of experience with the conflict in the Middle East would cause a lot of people to despair; but you never have given up hope, never lost sight of the ultimate goal of peace, and always considered it attainable. Someday, peace will come to the region, and it will be because of people like you, who never stop looking forward to a brighter tomorrow.

Hillary and I thank you for your friendship, and we wish you many more years of health, happiness, and wonderful accomplishments.

Sincerely,
Bill

From Israeli President and Former Prime Minister Shimon Peres

Shimon Peres

Danny Abraham defies definition. He is one of a kind. He is neither government, nor institution, nor organization, but goes beyond these to better this world. Danny achieves what governments are unable to do, conducting his own diplomacy, attending the courts of kings, presidents, and ministers, serving big powers. He achieves more than institutions, while *a priori* hating the things that are institutionalized, uncomfortable with all things ceremonial. Unlike organizations, he is free of bureaucracy. With his mobile phone in his pocket he conducts a whole network of contacts, decides on modes of action, and formulates plans.

Danny does all this in the service of peace and the improvement of people's lives. Danny loves Israel with all his being. He remains a Jew to his depth. Danny knows that there is no Israel without Judaism, but also no Judaism without Israel. Danny may live outside Israel, but he is never without Israel. . . . Evidence of his good work is spread all over Israel: a modern sports facility, a new university wing, a soccer field, and thankful families relieved of their distress.

Danny's life work has been the pursuit of peace between the Palestinians and us, between the Arab people and the Jewish people. To that end Danny spun ties and established relationships that could scarcely be deeper. These are ties and relationships that were hard to achieve and even harder to maintain. For this we are grateful. . . .

Danny takes in the world, living life to the full. He flies, sails, and travels the globe. Danny is full of love for this world and his family. He imparts to his children and grandchildren an enduring youthful spirit of mischief and the hard-earned wisdom of his life. Danny is inquisitive, has a sense of humor, and loves the company of people.

More than anything, Danny is a loyal friend. I would be hard-pressed to find a better friend than him. He is a steady friend in good times and bad. He retains his good spirit, even when evil winds blow across the world, keeping his faith in times of crises. For that we love him.

For years, Danny has been joking with me, dubbing me his "older brother" for the one year that separates . . . us. I therefore have the privilege of saying to Danny today, "My younger and beloved brother— one must cross the eighty-years mark to understand that the whole future is ahead of us.

Shimon Peres

From Former Israeli First Lady
Aura Herzog

Dearest Danny,

Of all the thousands of people that we know, and the dozens who are our friends, you are definitely a unique one—I would say the best friend Vivian [Chaim Herzog] and I had and have . . .

In the first meeting [we had], you encouraged Vivian to write an answer to all the Arab attacks at the UN that Israel was subjected to. It was a very great need at the time, and thus appeared the book *Who Stands Accused?*, which put Israel's case to the fore, with Vivian acknowledging your "invaluable practical support."

When Chaim was elected to the presidency, you came to the inauguration ceremony, and while we were having tea you disappeared and wandered upstairs, because you needed a band-aid, so you told me later. When you left, you mysteriously said to me, "Aura, you have a hell of a job to put this place right. You will hear from me." I could not guess what you meant. Sure enough, you initiated the Beautification Fund of the President's Residence, which enabled us and all future presidents to reside in a more functional, beautiful, and better-equipped environment—a real historic contribution . . .

Our friendship has lasted now for almost thirty years. We felt, and now I feel, blessed to have you as part of our lives. We salute you, our friend with a golden heart, amazingly clever and gifted, and such an exceptional "mensch."

Much love and continue
as you are.
Aura [Herzog]

246

From Isaac (Bougie) Herzog
(Former member of the Knesset and the Israeli cabinet, and Dan's lawyer in Israel)

Dear Danny,

You are a unique human being and it is not just a cliché. It dawned on me once, when in one of our . . . many heart-to-heart conversations you told me that "Indeed the more you give, the more you get." Only special people think and operate this way.

You make anyone who talks to you feel equal to you; you facilitate frankness and friendship; you are warm, gentle, and generous, in short you are incredible. Whenever I talk to you, I get a feeling that there is no age difference between us. I feel that you are from my generation—because you are so young in mind and spirit. I feel so very close to you in sad and happy moments. You were the first person I called when my dad passed away and it was not only because you were his best friend, but because *we* are best friends as well. I want to thank you for what I have learnt from you and the trust you have given me. You are indeed a true friend. . . .

So Mazel Tov, my true friend. Keep on with this great adventure, with Ewa, your children, and the wonderful family you have—and with all your friends who truly and totally love you.

Michal joins me with a huge kiss.

Love,
Isaac (Bougie) Herzog

From Former U. S. Secretary of State
Madeline Albright

Dear Danny,

I join with all your friends in wishing you a joyous 80th birthday.

Although others here worked hard, you stand alone in your commitment to bring peace to the Middle East. Your tireless optimism in the face of difficulties stands out. We all owe you a huge debt of gratitude.

I wish I had a photo of you and Sara Ehrman driving around Shepherdstown trying to find out what we were doing on the Syria track—but I don't so I just have it imprinted on my mind.

Thank you again for your dedication and being you. May you have many more years of good deeds and joy.

> With admiration and
> affection.
> Madeline

From Former U.S. National Security Advisor
Sandy Berger

Danny—

You are the youngest eighty-year-old I know. I think that is because you maintain your sense of passion— toward your family, your friends and to the causes you believe in, most notably peace in the Middle East.

During my years in the White House with President Clinton, there was *no one* more reliable, more steadfast or more unrelenting in bringing the parties in the region together than you.

It is work you carry on today.

Through all the obstacles, I truly believe that we will achieve an *end of conflict* and a *real peace —sooner* because of you.

> With love and respect,
> Sandy Berger

From U. S. Chief of Staff and Former U.S. Congressman Rahm Emanuel

Dear Danny,

I remember our first meeting in the Willard Hotel [in Washington, D.C.]. I thought I was hyperactive with an adult version of ADD. It was impossible to keep up with you as the conversation bounced from food to family, the Mideast to the Midwest.

From that moment forward I knew that I had met a kindred spirit. As I write this note I am at my D.C. office on a late night of votes. I am looking out on the Capitol, excited by the opportunities that are before me. Only in America. But much of what is before me is because of friends like you. Thank you for being a part of this journey. You are a real friend.

> Love and Peace
> Always,
> Rahm Emanuel

From H. Douglas Owens
(Son of the late Wayne Owens [D-Utah], Dan's close friend and partner in the pursuit of Middle East peace)

Dear Danny,

I am writing on behalf of my parents, Wayne and Marlene Owens. First, let me say, Happy Birthday! And many happy returns of the day!

Over the years, Mom and I have heard many stories about your work with Dad. You two were an amazing partnership. . . . There was the time you two were discussing the strategic importance of water in the Middle East and Israel. As I understand it, you, Dad, and some others were walking along, talking about the issue. Dad suggested that perhaps the water issue was different from other issues because it did not have close ties to history and religion. Unlike so many other issues, maybe there could be a neutral, technical solution to the water problem. Dad started talking about the possibility of a small, pilot desalination plant to see if the idea would work. Then you took a big leap in front of the others, turned around [to] them, and said, "No, not a small pilot plant. If we are going into it at all, we are going into it in a big way that will make a strategic difference. We'll promote a billion cubic meters." Others suggested that might not be realistic, but you said, "No baby steps." Well, the rest is history. You tackled the issue and now plants with 100 million cubic feet of capacity are in the works, Israel has endorsed a plan for a billion cubic meters, and you have been recognized as the groundbreaking visionary. You have real vision, Danny. Dad said you looked over the technicalities and went right to the strategic issues.

There were so many funny, happy stories we heard

about you too, Danny. You bringing an expensive bottle—was it Chivas Regal?—to Shimon Peres on his
birthday, and Dad having to keep either of you from
answering the phone for the rest of the day. Or the
time you showed the Crown Prince of Saudi Arabia the
photograph of your new daughter, and he asked, "What
is your diet?" . . . I also recall that Dad once lost his bag
and had to wear some of your clothes.

You and Dad were a unique duo in the world,
Danny. How I wish he were here to write you this letter. Godspeed as you carry on the good fight.

Very truly yours,
H. Douglas Owens

From Dan Rothem
*(Research Director for the Center for Middle East Peace
and Economic Cooperation)*

I remember once when Danny entered the car in
Jerusalem in the spring of 2004 after a troublesome
meeting with a chief Israeli executive. He was very
upset at the decision-making process regarding how to
overcome the political obstacles in promoting the disen-
gagement plan. It seems as if all else disappeared and
his only goal was to get the "gutless" leaders back on
track. That night, he called me up to his room at the
Hilton, and he was still upset over the day's events. I remember seeing him standing in his room, persistently
trying to figure out a way out of the mess. What resolve!

From Jihan "Gigi" Ghanim
(Executive Assistant at the Center for Middle East Peace)

After joining the Center for Middle East Peace two years ago, I remember all of my Arab friends telling me how awkward it might be to work for a Jewish boss when dealing with the Israeli-Palestinian conflict. I had to admit that initially I was a bit worried. After going to college in Egypt for three years, I was under the impression that there were only two sides to the conflict, and you could only be pro-Israeli or pro-Palestinian. These rigid definitions, I soon learned, were inadequate in defining a complex situation where human suffering is often forgotten in place of more rigid views of who is right and who is wrong. [But] after meeting Danny and seeing how much compassion and resolve he has toward ending this conflict, I couldn't help but question all of my preconceived notions about what it means to be Arab or Jewish in defining one's perspective. I am comforted by the fact that [at the Center for Middle East Peace] we all see the light no matter what our backgrounds are, and I am proud to be part of his continuous effort to make that light shine through in such difficult times.

From Moses Ratowsky
(President of Thompson Medical)

I first met Danny about fifty years ago. I had just married and there was never enough money, so I put an

252

ad in the local paper to prepare income tax returns. Danny answered my ad. I must say that when I first met him, Danny had a lot more hair and a lot less money than he does now. His records were in terrible shape, numbers written on scraps of paper. I can't remember what his income was then, but it was not much. What I do remember, even now, was the amount of money Danny gave to charity, many checks, but in small amounts. I thought that this man must have had a fine pair of parents.

When he asked how much he owed me, I was in a quandary. How much could I charge this poor soul? "Give me $15," I said. Dan promptly said, "That is not enough," and gave me $25.

I told him that if he was going to be a businessman he would need a set of books. Dan told me to set him up the proper way.

Thompson Medical Company was located then on the second floor over a paint store. Its product was an antiseptic ointment called San-Cura. How Danny got those drums of petrolatum, San-Cura's main ingredient, up those stairs, I'll never know. Mixed with chemicals, the product was bottled, and Danny sold the product to drugstores. It was tough going until Danny discovered the power of point of sales advertising and advertising in general, but that is another story.

In all the years we worked together, I can't remember words spoken in anger. I loved working with Danny, helping to build a business. Danny made me a better person.

I'll close by saying that Danny never knew that because of his generosity in paying me for preparing his income tax return, I made him a present of his first set of books.

From Dan Horwitz
(President of Thompson Medical Company)

My first lasting impression of you was in the early sixties when you and your band of "Merry Men" would invade Revco's buying offices with such conviction, belief and professional salesmanship, who could say no!

Perhaps the highlight of our relationship was your believing in me enough to ask me to head Thompson Medical Company. . . . Success in life can be measured in many ways; your financial success has been achieved by hard work and dedication to creating meaningful products for the world. Your most important success is measured by the thousands of people's lives you've personally touched by your kindness, sincerity, friendship and love.

Dianne and I are very proud to be a part of your life.

From Tom Kemeny
(Director, Thompson Medical Company Limited, UK)

I still remember standing with Dan in the early morning in the Lincoln Tower office building where we had our advertising facilities, interviewing people coming into the lobby. We were asking consumers which of two packs they would prefer and why, quite often riding up in the elevator with them while the interview was taking place. It wasn't a proper scientific sample, but somehow it seemed to work and we were getting very good insights. I was quite amazed at the sheer speed with which we could make a new drawing for a pack. We would change it many times, sometimes ten times in a few days. . . . We would then go out on the street and do what we called street intercepts, stopping consumers and asking which pack, which design, and which colors they preferred. Dan would always be there listening to consumers. I had great admiration for him and his commitment. Sure enough our efforts worked. When we finally found a pack that we felt had a chance, we would make a few dozen, put them in a store and do what we call a vitality test. If it sold one or two packs a week without advertising, we had a product, and then we would test-market it in one chain, one region. It was an amazing experience.

From Charles Noonan
(Vice-President, Thompson Medical Company)

Back in 1986, the company surprised Susie and me with a bridal shower. The shower was held in the lunchroom and when Danny entered, things became a little quiet. At that time, Susie was engaged in a conversation with Sylvia Fink, and not realizing who Danny was, continued speaking with Sylvia for a few more minutes. When they were done, Danny told Susie she was a lucky woman for marrying a man like me. She responded by saying, "Let me tell you" (at that point the room got really quiet), "he's the lucky one." Danny was so impressed with Susie's moxie and directness, he offered her a sales position. The truth is, Danny was right. Susie and I were both the lucky ones; eighteen years of marriage and three wonderful kids. But we were even luckier than that because we had Danny in our lives.

From Carl T. Tsang
(CFO, Slim-Fast Foods)

One memorable comment Danny made to me in the elevator at Phillips Point has forever made me a happier person. Danny said that I did not smile enough and therefore frequently came across as being upset about something. Danny helped me to smile when he told me to ask myself: "Are we smiling because we're happy or are we happy because we're smiling?" I now smile easily and feel happier.

From Monty Marsala
(Executive Assistant to Dr. Ed Steinberg, Vice-Chairman, Thompson Medical)

What was most outstanding was Danny's generosity to those who worked for him and at times to those who didn't. He rewarded us in every possible way. We worked hard and so did he, right beside us. Danny is a man of his word. He egged us on to do more and to do it better. We participated in every aspect of the companies—both Thompson Medical and Slim-Fast—and that is the way he wanted it because he constantly told us, "This is *our* company, and one day soon it will be a billion-dollar company." Well, Danny was wrong there, it turned out to be a $2.3 billion company. Danny would shower us with bonuses as if it were *our* company. He invented summer bonuses, and then, of course, there was the Thanksgiving bonus and, of course, the holiday parties that were held in the most interesting places in New York. We even had a summer party and a barbecue on a yacht no less. Danny showered us with good-heartedness and a feeling of togetherness you don't find in the everyday workplace. Danny is truly blessed and loved by those who have known him.

From Tim McCain
(Chief Investment Officer)

In recalling my first summer after Sarah and I moved to West Palm Beach, I remember one evening very fondly. I had to leave work early, not too early though (5:30), and as I said good-bye, I casually mentioned that I was leaving early because it was my anniversary. I vividly recall Danny's eyes lighting up as he stood up and said congratulations while pulling me aside. Handing me a $50 bill, he emphasized what a special day it was and how it should be celebrated:

champagne with peach nectar and flowers among other things. As Sarah and I sat on our back patio enjoying the champagne, we realized how lucky we both were to be a part of this organization that was such a reflection of Danny.

From Stephen Novick
(Vice-Chairman and Chief Creative Officer, Grey Global Group)

Simply put, Danny Abraham is the smartest guy I've ever met. He's also one of the nicest.

From Samuel Heyman
(Neighbor and Friend)

Danny set an important example in corporate America by proving that one can indeed operate a major company from a Palm Beach cabana.

From James Katzman
(Managing Director, Mergers & Acquisitions, Goldman Sachs)

There are two occasions in particular that I will no doubt always remember, both of which occurred while we were working on the sale of Slim-Fast. The first was when I called to tell Danny the price Unilever offered for the company [$2.3 billion]. We tracked Danny down on the boat, and after I told him the price he was speechless. In fact, word had it that he nearly fell off the deck. I asked him what he wanted to do and he told me to "Get it done," which we did. The second was that when we finalized the amount, he elected to pay all his employees bonuses. It is certainly unusual to pay bonuses to all employees in connection with a transaction [like this], and the fact that Danny felt it important to do so was [a testament] to his well-known generosity. He laid out certain guidelines, and following those guidelines we calculated the total bonus amount. It was a shocking sum, more than the total sales price for most companies. While the price for Slim-Fast was one of the highest paid for any business in the industry, Danny's generosity to his employees was even more remarkable.

From Rabbi Kenneth Brander
(Boca Raton Synagogue)

One of the most moving experiences that I had involving Danny may seem trivial, yet it has affected me, even to this day. It was during one of our first meetings, possibly the first time we met, in Palm Beach at Danny's home. We met in the lobby and walked to the cabana. As we were walking and discussing several different issues, Danny spotted a snail in the middle of the walkway. He stopped, picked up the snail, and put it in the bushes so that no one would crush it. This had a tremendous impact on me. I thought, here is a man who is involved in so many important charities, who has done so much good for the Jewish community as well as the world community. He is a man who interacts on a regular basis with world leaders, with prime ministers, presidents, members of Congress and the like. Yet, he took a moment to recognize that a snail might be crushed, and he lifted it with his hands and moved it to a safe place.

From Rabbi Haskel Lookstein
(Spiritual leader of Manhattan's Kehilat Jeshurun and Principal of the Ramaz School)

There was . . . something . . . that Dan did for us which has played a major role in the development of our school. In the early 1970s, we came to the conclusion that we needed to create an endowment fund at Ramaz. I believe that Dan was the first pledger to that fund. He gave us $100,000 to launch the fund. Subsequently, he gave us another $100,000 so that we were able to allocate every year one or two major scholarships. Today, thank God, that fund stands at approximately $15 million. I am not sure that this effort would ever have gotten off the ground were it not for the pioneer gift that he gave us.

From Rabbi Shlomo Riskin
(Chief Rabbi of Efrat in Israel and founder of the Lincoln Square Synagogue in New York)

Danny Abraham has been a beloved friend, a caring supporter and a wise mentor. The most outstanding incident that I can never forget is bound up with the most difficult decision I made in my life. My wife and I always dreamt of making *aliyah* to Israel. And when the opportunity of Efrat presented itself—although Efrat was then only an empty hill with a governmental promise of development into a city—I immediately announced that I was going on *aliyah*.

Danny asked to meet with me as soon as my announcement became official. He asked about my plans and showed profound understanding for the potential of what I was doing, although he warned me of the dangers. He supported my decision 100 percent, saying again and again that the leadership for the Jewish people had to emanate from Israel, and then, as he gave me a parting embrace, he told me, "Rabbi, I will never let you down. If ever you are in trouble, come to me."

If the period before *aliyah* was hectic, the period after was frightening and tumultuous. The streets of Efrat were not paved. The first winter was harsh, and we had neither heat nor electricity, and the Ministry of

Education, which had promised to supply the educational funding for the first Ohr Torah Stone School, Neveh Shmuel High School in Efrat, produced only a small fraction of what our expenses actually were. I learned only too quickly that you cannot draw money out of the bank unless you put money into the bank. I was forced to make my first fund-raising trip to America with a debt of $500,000, which meant that I would either raise the funds or be forced to abort my *aliyah*....

Then I remembered Danny's promise. I called for an appointment. Everyone knows that it isn't easy to track Danny down now, and it wasn't easy for me to track him down then. I called again and again. I was told that there would soon be a call back, but we never made contact. In utter frustration and as a very last hope, I went to his office and sat outside of it. When he came out the door, he greeted me like a long-lost son. We sat together, and he anxiously listened to all of my experiences and without being asked he gave me the kind of contribution that made it possible for me to return to Israel and to my family.

Danny is a loving and generous philanthropist. He is also a thinker who uses his funds to preserve Modern Orthodox Judaism throughout the world, and to sanctify God's name by showing that we are indeed a compassionate, humanitarian, and universalistic nation.

From Rabbi Avi Weiss
(Yeshivat Chovevei Torah Rabbinical School)

I remember once speaking in Palm Beach in the presence of Danny. I gave what I felt was a rather open, liberal talk on the politics of the Middle East. When I was finished, Danny looked at me and he said, "Good, you're getting there, but you're not quite there." That's Danny. In his own way, cajoling and teaching and pushing for what he powerfully believes in. Over the years, I have come to understand how passionately Danny seeks peace for all of humankind. Whatever one's political perspective, Danny's love of Israel and his pursuit of real shalom ought always to be respected.

And then there was the time I spent several hours with Danny at his Manhattan apartment. It was early morning and Danny was in his exercise attire, eating his healthy breakfast. Looking up at me, Danny launched into a loving talk. He reminded me that eating correctly is central. That's Danny—always teaching and encouraging others to stay well; always concerned with the welfare of the other.

From Rabbi Moshe Rom
(Dean, College for Advanced Halachic Studies)

Dan Abraham, a very precious person and my dear friend, is of priestly descent [a Kohen], and follows in the ways of his ancestor Aaron ha-Kohen, who "loved peace and pursued peace" (*Ethics of the Fathers* 1:12).

From David Altman
(Vice-President for Development, Netanya Academic College, Netanya, Israel)

I would like to relate an anecdote that sheds light on yet another wonderful aspect of Dan's character. When he received an honorary doctorate from Bar-Ilan University, he stood on the platform and greeted friends, family, and the dignitaries in the audience—which included all of Israel's leaders. Then he added, "I send a special greeting to my former wife, the mother of my children, for she gave me the greatest gift of all—our four wonderful daughters, who light up my life and give me the will and the ability to continue my efforts."

From Jim Hodge
(Mayo Foundation, Department of Development)

Dan came to Mayo Clinic as a patient and without prompting offered to provide healthy living centers for the benefit of Mayo staff. Last year alone there were 330,000 fitness visits at our Saint Mary's and Ozmun Dan Abraham Healthy Living Centers. Thus, Dan has given people a platform to improve their health and change their lives. In addition, his work to bring justice and a lasting peace to the Middle East has personally been an inspiration to me.

From Danny's Daughters Simmy, Tammy, Leah, and Rebecca—August 15, 2004

From Simmy

Dear Dad,

A few years back when I was in my ninth month with Sara Leah, I flew to France to be with you at your birthday party. When I returned to Ben Gurion Airport, a man came to help me through customs (and with my bags!). When he saw my name on my passport, he asked "Are you Danny Abraham's daughter?" I proudly replied, "Yes."

He then told me that once, when you came to Israel, he also helped you through customs—and he happened to say that the next day was both his wife's birthday and the day that he had to begin his army service. You immediately took out $100 from your pocket and with a warm smile, told the man to take out his wife to a special place for dinner that night. The man was so touched by your gesture—he hadn't forgotten it—and now he was elated to share it with me years later! When he told me this, my first reaction was "Yeah, that's my Dad!"

Today, when I think back to him telling me his story, I say to myself, "How many stories like this have I heard . . . ?"—and I know that they are only a fraction of the stories about you that people have to tell!!

I learn from you constantly and I pray that I will continue learning from you until well past 120!!

Dad, you are such an amazingly special man and I love you from the innermost part of my heart.

Happy 80th!!
Simmy

From Tammy

To My Dearest Dad, on the occasion of his 80th birthday,

The children of a father like you tell different stories than other kids do. Most dads work as lawyers, doctors, accountants, rabbis, or whatever. You have a different calling, and you have never missed a step in following it. I have watched in awe as you put every ounce of passion and energy to bring peace to Israel. A few funny stories of your adventures in international politics from your daughter's perspective:

I will never forget calling Karen [Shumilla] in the office a few years ago to find out where you were, only to turn on the television to CNN and see the funeral of Syrian President Hafez Assad with you standing next to Secretary of State Madeleine Albright, or our visit to the White House when you stood reading the entire Constitution in the Lincoln Bedroom as you kept President Clinton waiting for us downstairs at the dinner receiving line. I love the story you told me about the time you told Arafat to drop the fatigues and buy a suit. I don't think anyone else on the planet has had the courage to do that—I wish he would take your advice!

Also, did I ever get a chance to thank you for giving me, at the age of twenty-three, the opportunity to speak on your behalf at the inaugural ceremony of the S. Daniel Abraham School of Economics at Bar-Ilan University when I had to address almost the entire Israeli Knesset? Accidentally promoting Shimon Peres to Prime Minister from Foreign Minister in my introduction was one of the highlights of my career as your daughter and stand-in acceptance speaker. How about my first visit to the White House for President Reagan's state dinner in honor of President Herzog, when you made me stay, even after we found out we were not sitting together? It wasn't so bad as I sat next to Mr. Carlucci, a very nice man who spent thirty minutes asking me about my work, only to tell me his job was "Secretary of Defense" when I innocently asked, "So, what do you do?"

I have many memories from our work together at Thompson Medical and Slim-Fast, which bring a smile to my face whenever I think about them. Do you remember the many months I spent working on what I believed was our best commercial ever—the Way of Life—only to have you cancel the entire campaign after it aired for only two days? What about the two times you fired me and the one time I quit? Or, remember the October we decided to have 2,000 new products on the shelves by the end of the year, only to have two-thirds of them discontinued by the following season because we didn't have time to taste them all? But the truth is . . . you were always right. Your instincts never let you down, and you always stood by what you believed and earned everyone's respect. You cared about everybody at the company, knew them all by name, and always had a kind word and a smile for every employee, from the mailroom to the president. I remember everyone felt your positive energy and warmth whenever you walked into the office. The place came alive. And, with your amazingly generous heart, you always found a way to find a job for anyone who came to you for help or needed a start in business.

Through it all, you have been the best teacher anyone could have dreamed of, and I have grown and learned from watching you all these years. The unique way that you interpret ideas that seem so basic will always help me to view things from a fresh perspective. You are always there to help Carey with his challenges in business, and I love it when I get to watch you give him advice and share your wisdom with him.

We are both truly blessed to have you as a great mentor, and an even more wonderful father.

May we continue to celebrate many birthdays together to 120 and beyond!

Love Always,
Tammy

From Leah

Dearest Dad,

As I sat down to write this letter as a surprise for your special birthday, I started to think back about my years growing up with you.

One of my earliest memories is of the time shortly after we moved to Netanya. There had been a very bad accident across the street from our apartment. There was no ambulance service in Netanya at the time, and the nearest hospital was at least thirty minutes away. You put the seats down in the station wagon, and despite your aversion to blood, drove the injured to Hadera. Unfortunately, one of them didn't make it. As a result, you got involved in helping to start the hospital in Netanya. Other people might have just wallowed in sad thoughts or depression or would have tried to forget the whole thing, but you took the bull by the horns and did something amazing with it.

I was fortunate to grow up in a home with a father who always cared about people and still does! You instilled in us a very strong positive ethic of how to treat people, even if they wronged you. You never let anyone asking for money leave the house empty-handed, or without words of encouragement.

I remember going to visit Grandma in Long Beach during the summers when we were in the U.S. I loved the drives out there, especially when you would start telling us stories about what it was like to grow up there. You would talk about the "icebox," and scrounging bottle caps for redemption and being editor of the Long Beach newspaper. There was always a walk on the boardwalk, then Grandma's whole wheat bread and soup and, of course, tomatoes.

This brings me to our trips to Mahopac and the stops we would make at the roadside fresh veggie & fruit stands. You taught us how to pick out ripe tomatoes, corn, and melons. Later, in Netanya, there were also the trips on Friday to the shouk—also for the tomatoes, etc. We inevitably would come back with too much because all the produce looked and smelled too good to pass up.

It was always a special thing to me to watch you daven with your tallit and tefillin every morning. Maybe that's why I turned out the way I did.

You always tried to back us and help us in whatever way you could, especially if you thought that it was important to us. When I wanted to go back to Sharfman's for a second year, you backed me completely once you knew how important it was to me. On Pesach of my first year I came home with a whole new set of rules about how much matza and maror had to be eaten within a certain time frame (of either nine minutes or three, if you could do it). I was so nervous, but you were there for me—you even ate all the *shiurim* (measurements) right along with me. Everyone else thought that we were both crazy. You were amazing. You made me feel accepted and loved. That's what a daughter wants and thrives on. Thank you!

I'll always cherish that memory and all the other memories of your respect for the Torah and for great rabbis and how you always ran away from being honored. Your attitude was, "This is what I have to do—there's nothing great about it. It's what has to be done."

These attributes are not only the makings of a great father but of a great man as well. May we spend many, many more years together in health and happiness and love,

> Happy Birthday—All my
> love always,
> Leah

From Rebecca

Dear Dad,

I finally have half a minute to write how I feel to have an eighty-year-old dad. Well, we have another 120 to go, *Be'ezrat Hashem*.

We've learned a lot from you, Dad. To always be happy and try to have a smile for everyone. To always give without wanting to get. Babies are born with clenched fists and when people die their fists are open. But I guess you were never born with clenched fists. Anyway, I love you and you're the best dad anybody could ever have!!!

Love,
Rebecca

S. Daniel Abraham, a leading American entrepreneur and pioneer in both the pharmaceutical and diet food business, is the creator of Slim-Fast Foods, the most successful diet product in history. A well-known philanthropist, his gift to the Mayo Clinic served to create the Dan Abraham Healthy Living Center. He is also the founder of the Center for Middle Peace and Economic Cooperation in Washington, D.C.

Mr. Abraham was born on August 15, 1924, and raised in Long Beach, New York. He and his wife, Ewa, reside in Palm Beach with their daughter Sarah and son Sam. He also has four grown daughters, Rebecca, Leah, Tammy, and Simmy, twenty-six grandchildren, and three great-grandchildren.

Expanded edition of *Everything Is Possible: Life and Business Lessons from a Self-Made Billionaire and the Founder of Slim-Fast,* published by Newmarket Press, 2010 (ISBN: 978-1-55704-850-9).